MW01296026

A. P. Giannini
The Man with the Midas Touch

by

Dana Haight Cattani

Angela B. Haight

illustrated by

Natalie B. Christensen

authorHOUSE®

AuthorHouse™
1663 Liberty Drive, Suite 200
Bloomington, IN 47403
www.authorhouse.com
Phone: 1-800-839-8640

Text copyright © 2009 by Dana Haight Cattani and Angela B. Haight
Illustrations copyright © 2009 by Natalie B. Christensen
All rights reserved, etc.

No part of this book may be reproduced, stored in a retrieval system, or transmitted by any means without the written permission of the author.

First published by AuthorHouse 7/24/2009

ISBN: 978-1-4389-5492-9 (sc)
ISBN: 978-1-4389-5493-6 (hc)

Library of Congress Control Number: 2009904446

Printed in the United States of America
Bloomington, Indiana

This book is printed on acid-free paper.

To Kyle,
ballast and sail,
and to Angela, Peter, and Thomas,
fresh and fanciful breezes

—Dana Haight Cattani

With gratitude and love
to Robert R. Bowen and Bruce Haight
who taught me everything
I know about money,
and to Verona Angela Toronto Bowen,
who taught me to love all things Italian
and the written word

—Angela B. Haight

To Tyler,
who seems to make
everything
feel possible

—Natalie B. Christensen

CONTENTS

List of Illustrations

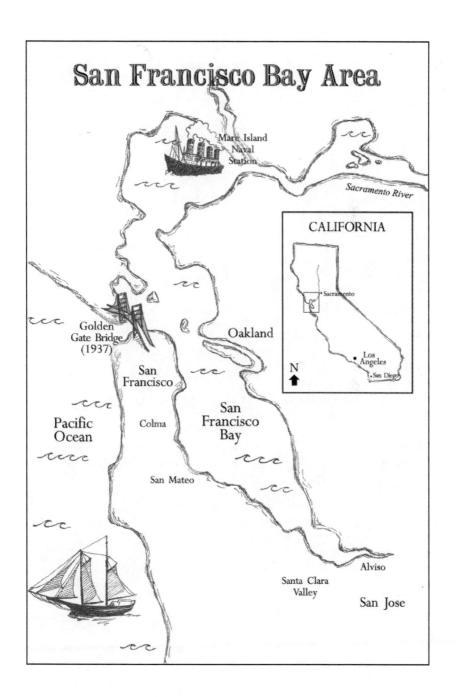

San Francisco Bay Area

Mare Island
Naval
Station

Sacramento River

CALIFORNIA

Sacramento

Los
Angeles

San Diego

N

Golden
Gate Bridge
(1937)

Oakland

San
Francisco

San
Francisco
Bay

Pacific
Ocean

Colma

San Mateo

Alviso

Santa Clara
Valley

San Jose

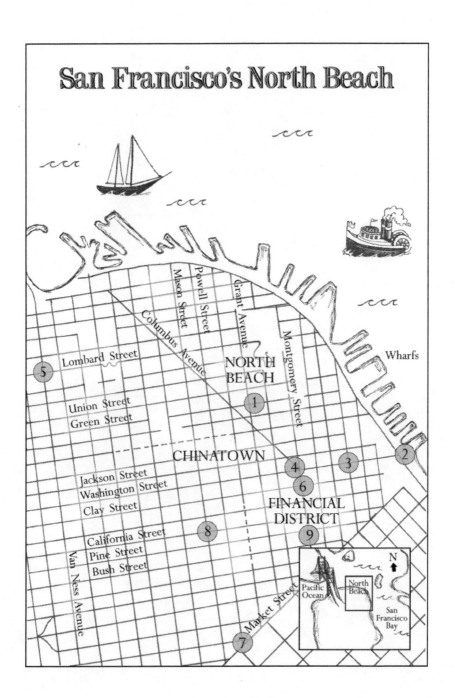

San Francisco's North Beach

North Beach

1. A. P.'s childhood home, 1884 (411 Green Street)
2. Washington Street Wharf
3. L. Scatena & Company (300 Washington Street)
4. Bank of Italy, 1904 (Corner of Washington Street and Columbus Avenue)
5. Dr. Attilio Giannini's home, 1906 (2745 Van Ness Avenue)
6. Bank of Italy, 1908 (Corner of Clay and Montgomery Streets)
7. Bank of Italy, 1921 (One Powell Street)
8. Pacific Union Club, Nob Hill (1000 California Street)
9. Bank of America, 1941 (300 Montgomery Street)

PREFACE

The ancient Greeks told stories about the fabled King Midas who turned everything he touched—an apple, a drinking cup, even a water fountain—into gold. Although A. P. Giannini did not have this mythical gift, he did make almost everything he touched more valuable. (From vegetables to movies to bridges, from unlikely political campaigns to struggling businesses, the projects A. P. backed usually succeeded. With remarkable skill, determination, and sometimes good luck, he achieved astounding results.)

No one would have guessed from his early life that Amadeo Peter Giannini (Ah-mah-DAY-o PE-ter Jee-ah-NEE-nee), the son of two uneducated immigrants, would become one of the world's most powerful men.

In 1864, his father, Luigi Giannini, had been enticed away from a small mountain village near Genoa, Italy, by exciting tales of gold lying on the ground in California. Like thousands before him, Luigi soon discovered that many of the stories he had heard in Italy were not true. Prospecting was lonely and dangerous. Only the luckiest found enough gold to avoid debt.

After five years in the gold fields, Luigi returned to Italy. He was through searching for gold, but he thought California would be a fine place to settle. Luigi wanted to marry. He had someone in mind, too—someone he had never met. Her name was Virginia DeMartini, and Luigi had worked alongside two of her brothers in the gold fields. When they read her lively and interesting letters out loud around the campfire, Luigi was charmed. He went back to Italy to meet her.

First Luigi had to convince Virginia's parents that he was a worthy suitor for their fifteen-year-old daughter. Her brothers' recommendations must have helped. The money belt filled with $20 gold pieces that he wore strapped to his chest also might have persuaded them that he was a hard worker with a proven ability to make his way in a new country. After obtaining her parents' approval, Luigi still had to convince Virginia. He must have been an excellent salesman, for after a six-week courtship, they were married in August of 1869. Luigi had brought a large white hat from America to offer to his bride, and she wore it for the wedding. The hat was the talk of the village. No one had seen anything like it before.

A few weeks later the newlyweds bought third-class tickets for America and sailed across the Atlantic. The transcontinental railroad had been completed recently, and they rode the train from New York to California. They settled in San Jose, a rough, bustling frontier town near the southern tip of San Francisco Bay.

Luigi used the last of his savings to lease a small two-story hotel. When word got out about the hotel's new management, Italian immigrants—mostly single young men who were working as farm hands or day laborers—flocked to board there. Like Luigi, they had come to work in the gold fields. They stayed because the warm, dry climate was similar to what they had known in Italy and the country seemed to promise success to ambitious, hard-working people.

However, many Anglo-Americans disliked and distrusted foreigners. Racial prejudice had led to the passage of some unfair laws. Occasionally there had been mob violence. The Chinese were the most frequent victims of prejudice, but Italians also received a share of the local hostility to strangers. Luigi and Virginia worked hard and tried to steer clear of trouble. They were preoccupied with events in their own lives, particularly the birth of their first son on May 6, 1870. They named him Amadeo Peter Giannini.

While working in the gold fields, Luigi had noticed the fine farmland in California. After two years in San Jose, he sold his lease on the hotel and bought 40 acres of orchard land in Alviso, a small town eight miles north. Railway lines and steamboats provided local farmers with ways to send their produce to markets all around San Francisco Bay.

In this favorable location and climate, the Giannini farm prospered. The family grew, too. Another son, Attilio, was born. Virginia and Luigi learned English, and Luigi became a United States citizen.

Then tragedy struck.

In August, 1876, Luigi hired a day laborer to help him pick fruit. After he was paid, the man claimed Luigi owed him two dollars more. A quarrel broke out, and the angry laborer left the farm. A week later he returned armed with a gun and shot Luigi.

Six-year-old Amadeo saw his father slump to the ground near the farmhouse. Luigi was able to tell the police about the disagreement and to name his assailant. Then he died.

Although the murderer was caught and sent to prison, the punishment did little to help Virginia Giannini. She was 22 years old, living on a large farm in a new country with no family nearby to help. To complicate matters further, she was pregnant. Her third child, George, was born six months after Luigi's death.

Life was hard for the young widow with three small children to raise and a farm to tend. For four years, she struggled to support the family by selling the artichokes, strawberries, and other specialty crops she had grown. Determined that her sons would get an education, she sent them to Alviso's one-room schoolhouse. Amadeo's classmates—who spoke Portuguese and Spanish, French and German, Armenian and Japanese and English—had trouble pronouncing his Italian name. They called him "Amador Jenning," but Amadeo didn't mind. He enjoyed school and made many friends.

Alviso's first schoolhouse where A. P. attended elementary school.
Reprinted with permission from Alviso, San Jose by Robert Burrill and Lynn Rogers. Available from the publisher online at www. arcadiapublishing.com or by calling 888-313-2665

In 1880, Virginia married Lorenzo Scatena, a produce hauler she had met on one of the steamboat trips she took to sell fruit in San Francisco. Lorenzo loved the Giannini boys, and they loved him. They called him "Pop." Lorenzo called Amadeo by his initials, A. P., a nickname that stuck for the rest of his life.

Virginia's trips to San Francisco convinced her that the city offered more opportunities for the family. Pop and Virginia sold the farm in Alviso and moved to North Beach, an Italian neighborhood in San Francisco close to the wharfs. Pop began a new job on the waterfront as a clerk for a produce company. His hard work earned significant profits for his employers. After a year, he asked for a raise. He received a smaller raise than he thought he deserved, so Virginia urged Pop to quit his job and start his own produce company. Surely they could do better.

Virginia DeMartini Giannini Scatena and Lorenzo Scatena,
A. P.'s mother and stepfather.
San Francisco History Center, San Francisco Public Library

I

SNEAKING OUT

1882
Jackson Street
San Francisco

A. P. Giannini tiptoed to the back door. He carried his shoes so he would not wake his mother. She would be furious if she caught her 12-year-old son sneaking out again, but A. P. could not resist following his stepfather, Pop, to work. About midnight, the paddle-wheel steamers began arriving at the Washington Street wharf, and A. P. wanted to be there.

He hurried through the darkened streets. When he reached the wharf, the docks buzzed with sound and activity. By the light of smoky oil lamps, workers unloaded crates of fruits and vegetables from the ships. Produce sellers hawked their goods in many languages. Pop carefully inspected the fruits and vegetables. He bargained for some of the best. Then he sold it to restaurants and grocery stores in the city.

A. P. wanted to help. Each ship carried a manifest, or list, of its cargo and passengers. When the steamers docked and the other traders were busy, A. P. copied each manifest in tidy penmanship for Pop. Once Pop knew exactly how much produce was available that night, he could decide how much to buy and how much to pay.

Night after night, A. P. watched attentively. He learned the names and faces of everyone on the wharf. Pop and his friends talked about freak storms and cold snaps, pests and drought. They complained about shortages, price gouging, and cheats. They celebrated bumper crops and bargains. They talked about the money they sometimes borrowed from the produce companies. A. P. breathed in all this information along with the chill night air.

When the sun rose, wagons carried off the produce, and the night's work was done. A. P. rushed home to eat. After breakfast, it was time for school. A. P.'s mother insisted that he learn to read and write in English. He did, and he was determined to be the best in his class. A. P. liked Washington Street Grammar School, but it was the Washington Street wharf that he loved.

II

TURNING ORANGES TO GOLD

1884
411 Green Street
San Francisco

Early one morning, A. P. woke to the muffled voices of his parents talking in the kitchen. He lay very still, trying to make out their words. He knew his mother was worried about him. She was busy with a toddler and new baby, but not too busy to worry about her three older sons. She thought A. P. was spending too much time at the wharf and neglecting his schoolwork. His afternoon naps and early nights were not enough sleep for a growing boy. How would he ever graduate from high school or college if he worked half the night and was too tired to study?

Pop had an idea. His business, L. Scatena & Company, had grown, and he and the family had moved into a new home. They were moving up in the world, and the house had a bay window with a view. Pop sold many kinds of local fruits and vegetables, including sugar beets, potatoes, corn, turnips, cantaloupes, pears, and plums. Oranges, however, were a luxury item. The best orange groves were hundreds of miles away in Southern California.

Pop told Virginia that he wanted to challenge A. P. to buy a boxcar of oranges from any farmer who was a new customer. It was difficult for experienced traders in San Francisco—much less a 14-year-old boy—to find and buy oranges. Pop said he would promise to buy A. P. a new gold watch if he could do it. Pop figured the task was nearly impossible and that A. P. would get discouraged with business and think more about school. A. P.'s mother thought the scheme might work.

When Pop presented the plan, A. P. pretended to be surprised. He accepted immediately. He loved a challenge, especially a difficult one.

A. P. spent his afternoons writing letters to farmers, promising fair prices and good service if they would sell to Pop's firm. Three weeks later, he handed Pop a contract for not just one, but two boxcar loads of oranges. Pop's plan had backfired, and A. P. had earned his gold watch.

A. P.'s mother was both proud of her ambitious son and distressed that he had succeeded. Would he ever finish school so he could make something of himself?

III

STICKING TO BUSINESS

1886
Sacramento River Valley
Central California

A. P. reigned in his horse on a hillside overlooking a farm, one of the biggest in the valley. After lunch, the sixteen-year-old hoped to sign a contract with the farmer who owned this land. A. P. dismounted and tied his horse to a tree. Sitting down in the shade, he pulled some bread and mozzarella cheese from his knapsack. He had not eaten since leaving a boarding house in Sacramento before dawn.

A. P. had met with several farmers already that morning. He asked lots of questions. What crops would they grow this year? How many acres? How was the soil? Were the trees ready to bear fruit yet? A. P. listened carefully. Would the farmers be interested in a contract to sell the harvest to L. Scatena & Company? Some were, and they signed agreements.

As he finished his lunch, A. P. noticed a cloud of dust far down the road. A team of horses was traveling toward the farm.

A. P. strained to see. He thought he recognized the rig from a rival produce firm. He stuffed the remaining bread and cheese into his knapsack and untied his horse. The long road to the farmhouse curved around a marsh, but A. P. cut across a field and rode straight to the muddy shore. He tethered his horse, stripped off his pants and shirt, and waded across, holding his clothes over his head. Dressing quickly, he hurried to the front door. By the time his competitor arrived, A. P. was negotiating a deal with the farmer.

At fifteen, A. P. had announced that he was quitting school to work full-time with Pop. To satisfy his disappointed mother, he enrolled in a three-month course in accounting at a local business college. Restless and eager to finish, he took the final exam after only six weeks, and he passed. He knew what he wanted to do and felt that there was no point in putting it off.

A. P. had good ideas and lots of them. He promised farmers payment in cash and on time. Pop honored those promises, and the farmers learned that they could expect honesty and integrity from L. Scatena & Company. They also could expect accuracy and attentive customer service. A. P. always remembered the farmers' names. In fact, he remembered the names of their wives and children. He also remembered dates and prices and quantities. This impressive memory won the confidence of potential customers and convinced many of them to do business with Pop's firm.

A. P. wanted to lay a foundation of trust and goodwill for L. Scatena & Company. To him, the work was not only about making that day's sales. He wanted to build relationships that would support Pop's business over time. New customers were important, but A. P. knew it was easier to keep existing customers happy than to find new ones. He tried to do both.

With Pop's approval, A. P. paid farmers in advance if they needed extra cash before their crops were ready to sell. If the farmers wanted to purchase more land or equipment, A. P. arranged for loans through the business. He hoped that their farms would thrive, and that they would remember that Pop's firm had been a steady partner in good times and bad.

A. P. was not always successful. In some small towns, farmers viewed him as an outsider. Competing merchants felt threatened by his interference in their territory. Sometimes they spread misleading rumors to harm his reputation. Although A. P. had been born in California, they said he was a foreigner. They hinted that as a Catholic, he must work for the Pope in Rome. They whispered that he had ties to Italian crime mobs. A. P. never responded publicly to these accusations. He stuck to business.

During the summer of 1887, A. P. became convinced that there were not enough pears growing that year to meet the demand during the fall season. He traveled throughout the Sacramento River Valley, making agreements with farmers to buy their crops. After a small harvest, the price of pears doubled. L. Scatena & Company earned $50,000 because A. P. had paid attention to a hunch. His timely action allowed him to help Pop's firm benefit from a shortage that surprised his competitors.

Earnings at L. Scatena & Company rose dramatically after A. P. started to work full-time. At the end of his first year, net profits were $10,000. The next year, they were $15,000. Two years later, net profits were nearly $100,000. Most of this growth came from business that A. P. had brought to the firm. He had purchased hundreds of tons of produce. He had brought in thousands of dollars in new business. In recognition of his importance to the firm, Pop made A. P. a partner when he was only 19 years old.

Besides the fertile agricultural areas of the Santa Clara and Sacramento Valleys, A. P. knew there was a vast opportunity farther away in the San Joaquin Valley and the Los Angeles basin. Other

San Francisco merchants had not ventured to trade much beyond a 200-mile radius from the city. However, the usual boundaries could not contain A. P.'s ambitions.

IV

COURTING CLORINDA

1892
North Beach
San Francisco

A. P. slipped quietly into a back pew of the old Spanish church. He lay his top hat and gloves down beside him and rested his cane carefully on the floor. He straightened his Prince Albert coat, nodding to his neighbors. They smiled in return. At six feet two and a half inches tall, with thick dark hair and a fashionable handlebar mustache, A. P. cut a fine figure around North Beach.

He also earned a good living. Pop's business was larger than ever, and A. P. continued to acquire new customers all over the state, including orange growers in tiny farming communities as far away as Hollywood, a few miles outside Los Angeles. He had been focused on the produce business since he was twelve years old, but he knew there was more to life than fruits and vegetables.

Mass began, and A. P. gazed around the church. In the choir, he spotted an attractive young woman. He glanced at her all through the service. When the mass ended, A. P. asked an older man sitting nearby who she was. Her name was Clorinda Agnes Cuneo, and she was the daughter of Joseph Cuneo, a wealthy North Beach resident.

Joseph Cuneo had immigrated from Italy to work in the California gold fields. After ten years, he opened a grocery store in North Beach. Although he never learned to read or write, he acquired numerous pieces of property and made a fortune in real estate. Clorinda, a well-known singer, was the youngest of his fourteen children.

A. P. wanted to court Clorinda, but there was one problem. She was already engaged. Her fiancé was a young doctor who was studying childhood diseases in Germany. They planned to marry as soon as he returned.

A. P. did not consider the absent fiancé a serious problem. He began a campaign to win Clorinda's affections. He showered her with flowers and candy. He planned picnics. He took her to the theater. In his beautiful penmanship, he wrote her passionate love letters.

Courting was exhausting. Sometimes A. P. took Clorinda home after a dance, changed from his black formal coat with long tails into his worn work clothes, and headed to the wharf to spend the rest of the night on business. He would have to sleep in the morning.

Clorinda was not immediately impressed by A. P. However, he was handsome and persistent, and he seemed to have a bright future. After three months of A. P.'s persuasive attentions, Clorinda broke off her engagement and agreed to marry him. Once again, A. P. had proven himself to be a determined competitor.

He and Clorinda were married on September 12, 1892, in Old St. Mary's Church. The newlyweds moved into a small frame house in North Beach not far from the waterfront. After a year of marriage, Clorinda gave birth to their first son. Over the next twelve years, four more sons and three daughters would join the family. A. P. loved Clorinda and the children, and he was happy with his personal life.

In his professional life, however, he began to feel restless.

V

BEATING BOSS BUCKLEY

October, 1899
New Charter Democratic Club
Corner of Union and Powell Streets
San Francisco

A. P. glanced over his shoulder. He wanted to be sure that no one was following him into the meeting. He did not want any of the thugs who worked for Blind Chris Buckley, the city's sightless but ruthless political boss, to bother him. He did not want them to bother his family at home on Green Street. He did not want thugs to bother anyone. A. P.'s active imagination often conjured up enemies to his business, but this time the enemies were real, and they were not afraid of violence.

The volunteers and local officials at this New Charter Democratic Club meeting were discouraged about their prospects in the upcoming election. Boss Buckley's men were determined to defeat any opponents. They threatened to hurt citizens who voted for other candidates. It was easy to know how someone voted because San Francisco did not use secret ballots. Given the dangers, many citizens simply did not vote.

The city had a well-deserved reputation for corruption. In the 44th Assembly District, which included North Beach, the deputy sheriff and the secretary of the Fire Commission controlled neighborhood life. Both were close associates of Boss Buckley. They offered five dollars to anyone who would vote for their friends in city elections. They demanded bribes and payments in exchange for not harming people or damaging their property. Paying bribes was expensive and discouraged new merchants. The neighborhood's bad reputation made it difficult for local business owners to secure loans. Bankers considered the area too risky. Corruption was bad for business.

A. P. believed that San Francisco needed honest leaders and reformed laws. Although he was busy at work, as the harvest season ended he made time to join the campaign to elect new leaders. Women could not vote at the time, so the focus of the campaign was only on men. A. P. organized the New Charter Democratic Club and rented a three-story building at Union and Powell Streets to serve as headquarters. He posted huge green and white signs advertising meetings. He strategized with local leaders and arranged for rallies at factories and shipyards where many men worked.

When candidates visited North Beach, A. P. introduced them to the crowds. Public speaking always made him nervous, but he was willing to do it for this important issue. Speaking in English or Italian, he explained how the reform candidates could improve neighborhood conditions. Many people were unhappy with city government, and they listened. They wanted change, too, but they were afraid to go to the polls and vote as they wished.

At the New Charter Democratic Club meeting, A. P. suggested a solution to this problem. He offered to pay for 75 wagons to drive men to the polls and deliver them safely home again. He called for volunteers with rifles to accompany the wagons and guard the district's polling places. Energized by his leadership and organization, many people offered to help. Boss Buckley's men had a plan, but now the reformers did, too.

On election day many North Beach citizens rode to the polls in the wagons. A. P. escorted some of the wagons himself. When the votes were counted, Boss Buckley's candidates had been defeated by majorities of six to one.

After the election, A. P. again walked the streets of North Beach, thanking supporters and handing out candy and cigars. In politics, as in business, he wanted people to be glad they had worked with him. However, A. P. did not want to run for office himself. He went back to the wharf. Business was booming. Refrigerated railroad cars now carried California produce across the country. So it was a shock when A. P. announced, at the age of 30, that he was going to move out of San Francisco to a suburb and retire.

VI

A New Career

Fall 1902
Columbus Savings and Loan Society
Corner of Washington Street
and Columbus Avenue
San Francisco

A. P.'s retirement was brief and ended abruptly. In 1902 Clorinda's father, Joseph Cuneo, died. Over the years, he had grown to like and trust A. P. In fact, Mr. Cuneo named A. P., the husband of his fourteenth child, as the executor of his will. A. P. was to be responsible for overseeing a large estate, which included cash, stocks, and more than one hundred properties. In addition to managing these family assets for his wife and her older siblings, A. P. inherited another role: board member at Columbus Savings and Loan Society, a North Beach bank.

Columbus Savings and Loan was an outgrowth of a successful travel agency started by John J. Fugazi in 1869. Mr. Fugazi represented a number of steamship and railroad lines with offices in the city. His agency served as an information bureau for Italian immigrants. Many of these recent immigrants preferred to conduct business in Italian, and they were slow to trust people outside their own ethnic community. Mr. Fugazi also had the only vault in North Beach. Many Italians kept their savings, passports, and other important papers in his safe. Sometimes they asked him to send money back to their families in Italy. He did, and in 1893, Mr. Fugazi officially opened Columbus Savings and Loan Society.

Nine years later, the other board members were delighted to have A. P. join them. He brought extensive business experience as well as a reputation for hard work and honesty. However, A. P. quickly found himself at odds with the others. At age 32, he was very confident and unaccustomed to making decisions with a group. He did not sit quietly and try to learn about banking from the older and more experienced board members as they expected.

Instead, A. P. asked pointed and uncomfortable questions. Why didn't the bank serve more people outside North Beach who were not Italian? Why were the loan policies so rigid? Why did they favor established businessmen and exclude new immigrants? Why did local banks lend millions of dollars for investments in London and Paris but not for the much smaller needs of ordinary San Franciscans? In fact, why run Columbus Savings and Loan like a bank when it could be run like a business? It could serve many more customers and be more profitable. A. P. tried to convince the others that the bank's policies were too cautious and overlooked opportunities for growth.

Heated arguments erupted in the meetings. The other board members resented the forceful way A. P. presented his ideas and found his proposals foolish. They had managed quite well before A. P. joined them and saw no reason to change. A. P. was strong-willed and impatient with those who saw the situation differently than he did. He could not, or would not, fit into someone else's vision.

When A. P. realized that the other directors were more concerned about avoiding risk than generating profit, he decided to turn his energies elsewhere. At a board meeting in the summer of 1904, he resigned his position. He left Columbus Savings and Loan and hurried to the Market Street office of his friend James Fagan, vice president of American National Bank. He had known A. P. for many years through his work with L. Scatena & Company. Mr. Fagan was sitting at his desk when A. P. burst into his office. "Giacomo," he announced, using the Italian name for James, "I'm going to start a bank. Tell me how to do it."

VII

BANK OF ITALY

October 17, 1904
Corner of Washington Street
and Columbus Avenue
San Francisco

A. P. did not hide from his previous associates. He rented a former saloon directly across the street from Columbus Savings and Loan Society and converted it into a tiny bank, which he called Bank of Italy. A. P. liked the location because it was a block from the police station. Day and night, the steady traffic of officers discouraged robberies, so the revolver he had bought for ten dollars could stay tucked in a drawer. The building was still in North Beach, but it was close to Chinatown, the financial district, and the wharfs, where many potential customers lived and worked.

A. P. started with $300,000 and a board of directors made up of local Italian businessmen, including five former directors from Columbus Savings and Loan. James Fagan, who brought extensive banking experience to the board, was the lone non-Italian. Each board member owned 100 shares of stock in the bank.

A. P. and the first Board of Directors of Bank of Italy, 1904.

Courtesy of The Bancroft Library, University of California, Berkeley

Shortly before A. P. started his bank, Columbus Savings and Loan Society had hired a new cashier, Armando Pedrini. A. P. also needed a cashier, and he offered to double Armando's salary if he would work for Bank of Italy instead. A. P. believed that Armando had qualities and skills that were worth the extra money. Armando had learned banking in Italy and South America before immigrating to San Francisco, and he spoke several languages. He knew what it was like to be a stranger in a new country. Armando was intelligent, polite, and charming. He gave a man in overalls the same attention and respect as a businessman in a suit.

That courtesy was important because A. P.'s Bank of Italy specialized in customers wearing overalls and hip boots and leather aprons. It catered to grocers, bakers, fish merchants, barbers, stone masons, shoemakers, and dock workers, some of whom could not speak or write English. Many had never used a bank before. They hid their extra coins at home in jars, cans, or mattresses. When they needed money, they went to loan sharks—back alley money-lenders who charged four or five times the prevailing interest rates but required little paperwork or collateral.

A. P. walked the streets and docks of North Beach, inviting people to deposit their savings in his bank. He explained that unlike jars or cans, a bank pays interest—a small amount of extra cash every month—for money it holds. Customers could earn money simply by having a deposit in a bank.

It sounded too good to be true. There must be a catch. However, earning money without labor appealed to people who did back-breaking, finger-numbing, leg-aching work every day. They listened to A. P. Many recognized him from the wharfs or the Boss Buckley campaign. He spoke their language. He remembered their faces and names. Those who were persuaded to try the bank discovered that A. P. also remembered exactly how much money each customer had deposited.

A. P., Armando, and the two other employees taught people how to fill out deposit slips and other forms. Unlike its competitors,

Bank of Italy was willing to accept small deposits and to make loans for as little as twenty-five dollars. People were more willing to deposit their money if they knew they could withdraw it easily. A. P. believed that some of the poor immigrants who used his bank would prosper eventually. He wanted their good will now, but he also hoped to build a loyal base of customers for the future.

At the end of the first day of business, Bank of Italy had accepted deposits of $8,780. The largest deposit came from a dozen North Beach fish merchants who each opened savings accounts. A. P.'s mother deposited $1,000 on the second day of business along with his sister-in-law and his employees. It was a start.

Over the next year, A. P. revisited farmers he knew in the Sacramento and Santa Clara Valleys to tell them about his new bank. He worked long hours. Customers often wandered by the bank at night or on weekends to find A. P. or another employee there working. The doors were rarely locked.

Not many San Francisco bankers paid any attention to Bank of Italy. If they noticed it at all, they were disdainful of its small but loyal base of working-class Italians. It was certainly no threat to the bigger banks with their wealthy and powerful customers.

A. P.'s customers were neither wealthy nor powerful. They could not qualify for loans from big banks. However, at Bank of Italy, a person did not need to have money in order to get money. A. P. made many "character loans" to friends and neighbors who had little collateral but his personal knowledge of their good names and reputations. Customers lined up to meet with him. When he offered to sell stock in his bank to the public, so many North Beach residents wanted to buy it that A. P. asked the board members to sell some of their shares. He wanted as many people as possible to have a stake in the success of his bank. Through careful and determined effort, A. P.'s bank was growing and poised for the future. He was pleased, but he could not have guessed that the immediate future would be so swift and devastating.

VIII

The Inferno

Wednesday, April 18, 1906
San Francisco

Shortly after 5 a. m. the deep rumbles began. Moments later a violent earthquake rocked San Francisco. The quake lasted just 28 seconds, but its effects would be felt for years.

People were tossed from their beds. Street car tracks twisted and chimneys crumbled. Windows shattered. The new San Francisco City Hall collapsed. Buildings constructed on soft soil near the bay trembled and slipped from their foundations.

When the earthquake struck, Fire Chief Dennis Sullivan lay sleeping in his room on the third floor of his official residence on Bush Street. The two floors below housed the firemen of Engine Company 2. Jumping up, Chief Sullivan ran to check on his wife who was sleeping in a nearby room. Before he could reach her, towering brick smokestacks on the California Hotel next door crashed through the roof of the fire house and 60 feet down into the cellar. Both the Sullivans were buried in the rubble. When the firefighters found them, Mrs. Sullivan was only slightly hurt, but the chief was seriously injured and unconscious. As the firemen carried him to the hospital, wisps of smoke already trailed up from fires in nearby buildings. An inferno was about to break loose in the largest city in the West, where 400,000 people lived side-by-side, many in cheap wooden housing.

No fire alarms sounded that morning in the city. The alarm system, located in a small building in Chinatown, consisted of glass jars holding wet cells, or batteries. At the first trembling of the earthquake, the jars toppled to the floor and fractured into jagged shards. Fortunately, no alarms were needed. Everyone was awake, and rising clouds of smoke told the story. Tangled electrical wires, overturned stoves, and broken gas pipes ignited fires all around the city. Hot embers spread the flames.

Chief Sullivan long had been concerned about the water supply in the event of a major fire. The young city of San Francisco had experienced six devastating blazes already. The chief had battled for years to get a supplementary salt-water system and to improve huge cisterns that had been built decades before under city streets. However, local political leaders had other priorities. San Francisco was surrounded on three sides by water, they said. How could the city ever need more?

As soon as the firemen could hitch their frightened horses to the old steam pumping engines, they headed for the nearest blaze. The earthquake had cracked and split many water pipes. Some were empty. Others shot geysers thirty feet into the air, flooding the streets. Equipment was buried in rubble, and many streets were impassable. Water from the few working hydrants, cisterns, and sewers was not enough. Hoses were rigged to draw water from San Francisco Bay. This effort saved the waterfront and the wharfs, but it was not helpful farther away.

San Francisco Fire Department's Engine #3, 1906.
San Francisco History Center, San Francisco Public Library

Many sturdy buildings in the business district were intact after the earthquake and had little damage because they were built on relatively stable land. By contrast, the houses south of Market Street stood on filled land, former bay marshes and tidal flats that had been packed with soil to create new ground. Some houses dated from the time of the Forty-Niners, prospectors who came to California during the gold rush of 1849 and hurriedly built temporary housing. These flimsy structures fell immediately, and the piles of broken lumber provided fodder for the flames. North of Market Street, 20,000 Chinese lived crowded into five square blocks, confined by invisible walls of prejudice. Their shoddy tenements also burned rapidly as the fires consumed what the earthquake had left behind.

```
┌─────────────────────────────────────────────┐
│                                               │
│              TELEGRAM                         │
│                                               │
│   EARTHQUAKE.  TOWN ON FIRE.  SEND MARINES    │
│   AND TUGS.                                    │
│                                               │
└─────────────────────────────────────────────┘
```

Telegram from San Francisco Mayor Eugene Schmitz to the
naval station at nearby Mare Island, April 18, 1906

```
┌─────────────────────────────────────────────┐
│                                               │
│              TELEGRAM                         │
│                                               │
│   SEND FIRE ENGINES, HOSE, ALSO DYNAMITE,     │
│   IMMEDIATELY.                                 │
│                                               │
└─────────────────────────────────────────────┘
```

Telegram from San Francisco Mayor Eugene Schmitz to
Oakland Mayor Frank Mott, April 18, 1906

The Mayor of San Francisco, Eugene Schmitz, met with the police commissioners and immediately ordered every saloon in town to close. They had enough problems without drunkenness. Mayor Schmitz appointed a Committee of Safety, which consisted of 50 prominent citizens, to help him respond to the crisis. He also sent urgent telegrams to the Mayor of Oakland, across the bay, and to Mare Island Naval Station.

```
┌ ─ ─ ─ ─ ─ ─ ─ ─ ─ ─ ─ ─ ─ ─ ─ ─ ┐
│                                  │
│          TELEGRAM                │
│                                  │
│  THEY ARE BLOWING UP STANDING BUILDINGS │
│  THAT ARE IN THE PATH OF FLAMES WITH    │
│  DYNAMITE.  NO WATER.  IT S AWFUL.  THERE │
│  IS NO COMMUNICATION ANYWHERE AND       │
│  ENTIRE PHONE SYSTEM BUSTED.            │
│                                  │
└ ─ ─ ─ ─ ─ ─ ─ ─ ─ ─ ─ ─ ─ ─ ─ ─ ┘
```

Telegram from the chief operator of the Postal-Telegraph Cable
Company in San Francisco to his New York office at 2:20 p.m.
on April 18, 1906

```
┌ ─ ─ ─ ─ ─ ─ ─ ─ ─ ─ ─ ─ ─ ─ ─ ─ ┐
│                                  │
│          TELEGRAM                │
│                                  │
│  FOOD IS VERY SCARCE.  PRICES MORE THAN │
│  DOUBLED.  WATER CAN HARDLY BE OBTAINED │
│  EVEN FOR DRINKING PURPOSES.  THE ENTIRE │
│  CITY WITH NO EXCEPTION IS DOOMED.  GOLDEN │
│  GATE PARK ONE VAST HOSPITAL.           │
│                                  │
└ ─ ─ ─ ─ ─ ─ ─ ─ ─ ─ ─ ─ ─ ─ ─ ─ ┘
```

Telegram from the chief operator of the Postal-Telegraph Cable
Company (sent from a station on Goat Island in San Francisco
Bay) to his New York office at 10:25 a.m. on April 19, 1906

TELEGRAM

FIRE IS STILL RAGING IN SAN FRANCISCO...
THE FIRE CANNOT BE CHECKED UNTIL IT
BURNS OUT. EVERY BUILDING IN BUSINESS
SECTION AND NEARLY HALF OF RESIDENCE
SECTION DESTROYED NOW AND NOT A LARGE
BUILDING LEFT STANDING.

Telegram sent from Oakland on April 19, 1906

San Francisco City Hall, 1906, before the earthquake.
San Francisco History Center, San Francisco Public Library

San Francisco City Hall, 1906, after the earthquake.
San Francisco History Center, San Francisco Public Library

Chief of Police Jeremiah Dinan issued orders to shoot looters on sight, and Mayor Schmitz reinforced this threat with a proclamation of his own.

PROCLAMATION
By the Mayor

The Federal Troops, the members of the Regular Police Force, and all Special Police Officers have been authorized by me to kill any and all persons found engaging in Looting or in the Commission of Any Other Crime.

I have directed all the Gas and Electric Lighting Companies not to turn on Gas or Electricity until I order them to do so. You may therefore expect the city to remain in darkness for an indefinite time.

I request all citizens to remain at home from darkness until daylight every night until order is restored.

I warn all Citizens of the danger of fire from Damaged or Destroyed Chimneys, Broken or Leaking Gas Pipes or Fixtures, or any like cause.

E. E. Schmitz, Mayor
Dated April 18, 1906

The Mayor ordered the Chief of Police to have 5,000 copies of this proclamation printed at a shop on the outskirts of the city and distributed during the afternoon of April 18, 1906.

Crowds of frightened people gathered in the streets. Many clutched blankets, food, or a few prized belongings. The ground still trembled and smoke obscured the sun. People streamed down Market Street, hoping to catch the ferry to Oakland. Some gathered at Union Square, a park in the city's center, but many people fled to nearby hills to watch the spectacle, or to Golden Gate Park or other smaller city parks. Tent cities soon sprang up. As before the earthquake, the Chinese were separate from all other San Franciscans in their own refugee camps.

People carried all they could salvage from their homes, pushing or pulling steamer trunks, wheelbarrows, or wagons loaded with bird cages, victrolas, banjos, tubs, mirrors, sewing machines, portraits, even upright pianos. Behind them, looters darted into abandoned offices and homes, grabbing anything of value.

Wild rumors spread quickly. "Chicago is under water." "Seattle and Portland have been wiped out by a tidal wave." "Los Angeles has been destroyed by a quake." Official communication was slow and unreliable. Within the city, telephone and electricity lines were broken. Messages could be relayed only by people on foot or on horseback.

Brigadier General Frederick Funston was the highest ranking Army officer in San Francisco. He left his apartment shortly after the earthquake and hurried to Nob Hill to survey the damage. He decided troops would be needed to protect government property and to help the police and firemen maintain order. Funston ran to the Army stables on Pine Street and dispatched a messenger to the commander at Fort Mason to send all available men to report to Police Chief Dinan.

The troops arrived on Market Street before 7 a. m. carrying rifles with fixed bayonets. They were joined at 8 a. m. by more troops from the Presidio, another large military base under Funston's control. With no time or means of consulting with his commanding officers, Funston had to make decisions alone and quickly. After the crisis was over, he sent a telegram recounting his actions to William Howard Taft, the Secretary of War, which concluded hopefully, "I shall expect to receive the necessary authority."

While newspapers claimed later that between 20 and 100 people had been shot on the streets, often for slight infractions, General Funston said that only two killings had been reported to him. The behavior of some soldiers did cause public criticism, but Funston's swift action in gathering soldiers to assist the police and volunteer patrolmen helped to avoid serious crime and mass panic.

Twenty hours after the earthquake, fire had destroyed most of the financial district of San Francisco. All of the area south of Market Street had burned, as well as Chinatown and the Hayes Valley. Over 100,000 people were homeless. Three days later, Fire Chief Dennis Sullivan died without knowing that the tragedy he had hoped to avoid had become grim reality.

IX

THE ESCAPE

April 18, 1906
San Francisco

San Francisco was not alone in its agony. The earthquake had reverberated through towns from Fort Bragg, nearly 200 miles north, to Salinas, 100 miles south. Pockets of devastation and ruin dotted an area 40 miles wide along the California coast.

In their San Mateo home, 17 miles south of San Francisco, the Gianninis were jolted from their beds when the quake struck. The chimney of their home collapsed and took part of the roof tumbling to the ground with it. The house was shaken to its foundation but sustained no additional damage.

Clorinda Giannini was expecting her eighth child. A. P. tried to calm and comfort her and the children. Then he dressed quickly, arranged with neighbors to look in on his family, and hurried to the train station. A noisy crowd was milling about hoping that a train would come. At last one did, and A. P. boarded with other people anxious about their relatives, friends, and businesses, as well as gawkers in search of a spectacle. The train crawled along with frequent unscheduled stops. Finally, it could go no farther. It stopped at the old station at 22ⁿᵈ and Valencia Streets, several miles from North Beach. A. P. bounded from the train and set out on foot for the bank.

Armando Pedrini, Bank of Italy's cashier, had begun the day as he always did with a trip to the strong and well-guarded vaults at nearby Crocker-Woolworth National, San Francisco's largest bank. Even with a police station nearby, A. P. did not like to keep money overnight in his bank. His iron safe looked secure to customers, but it was really not much more than a large tin box. In the evenings, Armando took the money to the bigger bank for safekeeping.

After retrieving $80,000 from Crocker-Woolworth that morning, Armando returned to Bank of Italy and placed the money—mostly gold and silver—in its safe. Although A. P. had not arrived, Armando opened the bank for business by nine o'clock with the day's cash on hand. He stood at the door and waited for customers. Yet all morning, the three wooden desks and few chairs inside the one-room bank remained empty. Built on solid ground, the bank had only minor damage from the earthquake, but Armando could see dark clouds of smoke drifting overhead, spreading burning cinders like dandelion seeds.

About noon, A. P. came hurrying up the street. He had spent five hours trying to get to work instead of his usual 30 minutes. He sent Armando out in search of news and information. Loud explosions began to jar the city. Working ahead of the flames, soldiers and firemen tried to create a fire line by deliberately blowing up buildings with dynamite. They hoped that without wood structures or other fuel, the fires would not be able to spread.

Instead, their efforts added to the chaos. The explosions blew out windows, raining shards of glass, marble, brick, and concrete into the streets. Errant blasts set new buildings on fire. With too many fires and not enough experienced men, efforts to draw a line against the advancing blaze proved futile. The fire front was a mile wide, and the few steam engines and hook-and-ladders could not travel quickly through the wreckage. With no reliable communication, no water, and no leadership from their dying chief, the 585 San Francisco firefighters faced impossible odds of saving their city.

By early afternoon, A. P. saw that the giant fire south of Market Street was heading toward North Beach. Quickly, he closed the bank. Believing that no place in San Francisco was safe, A. P. decided to take the money to his home.

But how? The streets were clogged with rubble. Gangs of ruffians wandered about, looking for trouble. No trains or street cars could operate. All the firemen, soldiers, and police were working desperately to control the fires. A. P. had to carry tens of thousands of dollars in gold and silver through a dangerous and fiery city. He needed to camouflage his valuable cargo, but he would have to hide it in plain sight.

Hurriedly, A. P. sent for two wagons and teams of horses from L. Scatena & Company. With the help of Armando and Clorinda's brother, Clarence Cuneo, A. P. loaded the bags of gold and silver into the wagons and covered them with crates of oranges. Behind Babe and Chub, the lead horses, the men drove to the Cuneo home at the far end of North Beach. There they piled mattresses on top of the orange crates so that the wagons looked like all the other carts, wheelbarrows, and baby carriages in the city loaded down with people's belongings. The men ate a quick supper at Clarence's house and waited until the late afternoon sun, burning through a smoky haze, had set. When it was finally dark, they began the risky journey out of San Francisco. An estimated 6.5 billion bricks had fallen during the earthquake and fire. So much debris clogged the streets that it took the horses all night to travel the 17 miles to A. P.'s house. He was relieved to get there, but he still did not feel safe. A. P. hid the gold and silver in the ash pit of the living room fireplace. The men stood guard around the house. They hardly slept the next day and night, but all was quiet.

X

THE BANK ON THE WHARF

Friday, April 20, 1906
Washington Street Wharf
San Francisco

For three days the fires raged. When A. P. returned to San Francisco on April 20, he found thousands of people living in tents and temporary shelters. Restaurants, theaters, libraries, courts, and jails had disappeared along with thirty schools, eighty churches and convents, and 250,000 homes. At least 450 people had died. Nearly 500 blocks had burned—a third of the city—including most of North Beach. Although his Bank of Italy had survived the earthquake, it had been destroyed by the fire. All that remained of its safe was a lump of molten iron.

Most of the city's banks, including the Crocker-Woolworth, had burned. Their fire-proof vaults were so sizzling hot that it might be days or even weeks before they could be opened. Bank officers feared that if the vaults were opened before the inside had cooled, the rush of fresh oxygen could ignite any paper currency or important documents. The money was trapped.

North Beach, with Alcatraz Island in the distance,
before the 1906 earthquake.
San Francisco History Center, San Francisco Public Library

North Beach after the 1906 earthquake and fire.
San Francisco History Center, San Francisco Public Library

On April 19, California Governor George Pardee had declared a bank holiday. He wanted to prevent a run on the banks and to give the officers more time to meet their customers' needs in an orderly way. Some bankers wanted to wait thirty days before opening for business. By then, they hoped that insurance companies would begin paying claims for damaged property so that customers would not need to withdraw as much money at once.

San Francisco Chronicle
April 22, 1906

"There is plenty of money here, but it will take some time to prepare for business. It is useless to begin to do business until we are prepared. We cannot pay out money until we have a place to pay it from," according to banking committee chairman Homer King.

San Francisco Examiner
April 27, 1906

The bankers repeat their statement that they will relieve the wants of their depositors at the earliest possible time, but have not yet reached any conclusion as to how or when they can do so.

A. P. did not want to wait. Some of his customers had no food, no homes, and no jobs. They did not want to be told that for the next thirty days they would have no cash, either. On April 27, the same day the *Examiner* reported that the bankers still had no plan for resuming business, A. P. placed a boxed advertisement of his own in the *San Francisco Chronicle*, which was temporarily published in Oakland. He wanted his customers—and everyone else—to know that his bank was open. The money was safe and available for people to rebuild their homes and businesses. The bank building had burned, but the Van Ness Avenue home of A. P.'s brother, Dr. Attilio Giannini, had escaped the fire. This house would be the bank's main office.

San Francisco Chronicle
April 27, 1906

BANK OF ITALY

Temporarily Located at
2745 Van Ness Avenue
Corner Lombard St.

The bank also would have a temporary desk at the Washington Street wharf, closer to North Beach. With his usual dramatic flair, A. P. set up shop near the fire's greatest devastation and at the waterfront where food and supplies would arrive first. He knew that people would be there, and he wanted to be there, too.

The bank on the wharf was little more than two barrels with a plank resting between them. On top of this makeshift desk, A. P. dropped a heavy bag of gold. It clinked and jangled. Behind the barrels, he hung a handmade Bank of Italy sign. A. P. made optimistic predictions about the city's future to anyone within earshot of his booming voice. He and the gold were a welcome and reassuring sight.

Word of the open-air bank spread quickly in North Beach. Nervous customers began to arrive. Would A. P. remember them? He greeted them by name. He knew how much money they had in his bank. He knew what it would cost them to rebuild.

A. P. brought money every day from the fireplace stash at his home to the bank on the wharf. His customers came, and so did their friends and neighbors and relatives. The money still smelled like oranges from its wagon ride through the burning city, but no one seemed to mind.

XI

Business as Usual

May, 1906
632 Montgomery Street
San Francisco

A line of people curved out the front door of Bank of Italy. Three weeks after the earthquake, the bank on the wharf had moved indoors. A. P. rented a surviving office on Montgomery Street, just a few blocks away from the burned-out remains of the original Bank of Italy. He set up his desk, and the people followed.

Many of them needed loans, of course. People wanted to buy lumber and other construction supplies to rebuild. They needed food, clothing, tools, horses, and wagons. The requests for money far exceeded the available supply. So, when people applied for loans, A. P. asked them to raise half the amount they wanted on their own. He knew that many people, especially immigrants, did not trust banks and kept their money hidden. Some had hoarded gold for years. After his customers had raided their secret hiding places and borrowed from friends or relatives, A. P. considered their requests. With a handshake, he approved many loans to old customers and new ones. By asking people to help locate and use available funds in the community, A. P. was able to make many loans without letting the bank run out of money.

𝕾𝖆𝖓 𝕵𝖗𝖆𝖓𝖈𝖎𝖘𝖈𝖔 𝕰𝖝𝖆𝖒𝖎𝖓𝖊𝖗
𝕸𝖆𝖞 22, 1906

BANK OF ITALY

632 Montgomery Street
(Montgomery Block)
NOW OPEN
FOR REGULAR BUSINESS
Absolutely no loss suffered by
reason of the recent disaster.

In fact, the bank was growing. Many people came to Bank of Italy not to borrow but to deposit money. Some were refugees living in tents or temporary camps with little privacy or security for their belongings. In these conditions, money hidden in jars or mattresses easily could be lost or stolen. Many people concluded that their money might be safer in a bank. Those who brought their savings to Bank of Italy found A. P., confident and inspiring, ready to accept their new deposits. Six weeks after the earthquake, people were depositing more money than they were withdrawing from Bank of Italy. In spite of the disaster, the number of savings accounts at the bank doubled in 1906.

While the city was still smoldering, A. P. found ship captains and loaned them money to purchase wood from Oregon and Washington. Knowing that lumber was in great demand, he might have made a profit for himself, but he did not. Instead,

A. P. used some of the bank's money to bring building materials to the city. The ship captains generally had the lumber sold even before docking in San Francisco. They benefited from A. P.'s foresight, as did the people who bought the lumber. The price of building materials skyrocketed later that year. During the next few months, an irregular drumming of saws, drills, and hammers beat out across the city. With lumber and loans, many from Bank of Italy, North Beach was one of the first neighborhoods in the city to rebuild.

Outside of California, the scope of the catastrophe shocked the nation. The Senate voted to send $500,000 in relief, but the House of Representatives raised that figure to $1 million. Supplies poured in from all over the United States.

XII

Staying Calm in a Panic

January, 1907
New York City

Just months after the earthquake, Bank of Italy was doing so well that A. P. decided he could take Clorinda on a vacation. It was their first big trip away after fifteen years of marriage. A. P. chose New York, the banking capital of the United States, as their destination. Even on vacation, he was thinking about business.

Just as he had done when he was a young man traveling among farms and buying produce, A. P. made a plan. He wanted to meet with other bankers and with prominent Italian businessmen. He wanted to question them about conditions, trends, and future prospects. He wanted to learn more about banking outside of San Francisco. Homes and buildings were rising from the rubble in North Beach. A. P. wanted fresh ideas and goals to guide his bank in this new environment.

However, A. P. was alarmed by the information he gathered. New York bankers were worried. Their banks were doing well, but the men were uneasy about the small reserves of gold in their vaults. Customers expected to be able to withdraw their money in gold at any time.

Many people did not consider paper money to be as valuable as gold coins, especially in times of uncertainty. Paper money suddenly could become less valuable if the government printed more or changed its policies. For this reason, California law required that tax payments could only be made in gold. Ordinary citizens had good reason to be skeptical of a national currency that their own state government did not trust.

Unlike paper, gold itself had significant value as a precious metal. The world supply of gold was limited, and it could not be printed or manufactured. Gold was the most trusted and reliable currency of the day, and it was up to the banks to keep enough on hand for their customers.

How much was enough? By law, banks were required to keep 25% of their deposits as reserves. The rest could be loaned. Making loans was profitable because the borrower paid interest to the bank. Keeping reserves was not as profitable because the bank had to pay the interest to the depositor. Since loans earned more money than reserves, bankers had an incentive to ignore the 25% reserve requirement. Some did lend out more money than was allowed. If reserves fell a little low, the bankers would borrow from another bank that kept more reserves. There would be no real consequences unless too many bankers ignored the requirement, lots of customers suddenly demanded their deposits back, and the banks ran out of gold.

After talking to a number of bankers, A. P. concluded that gold reserves in New York were dangerously low. The banks were like a house of cards that even a gentle wind could topple. News of one bank failure would send worried customers crowding into other banks, demanding their savings. If most of the banks had loaned too much money, there could be a panic. A. P. was so anxious about this prospect that he booked train tickets back to

San Francisco. Cutting their vacation short, he and Clorinda started home.

Back in North Beach, A. P. began a quiet campaign to boost Bank of Italy's gold reserves. He increased deposits by recruiting new customers so that more money was coming into the bank. He dramatically decreased the number of loans so that less money was going out. He exchanged the bank's paper money for gold whenever possible. A. P. instructed the bank tellers to pay out paper money unless a customer specifically requested gold.

When Clarence Cuneo deposited Bank of Italy money in Crocker-Woolworth National Bank every night, A. P. was supposed to send a certain percent in gold. His friend James Fagan, now a vice-president at Crocker-Woolworth and still a director at Bank of Italy, scoffed at A. P.'s plans to secure more gold reserves. Since Mr. Fagan was unconcerned, A. P. substituted more paper and less gold in the nightly deposit. The amount of the deposit was the same, and the switch made little difference to a big bank like Crocker-Woolworth. The little Bank of Italy's gold reserves grew.

In October, 1907, prices on the New York Stock Exchange plummeted. Worried customers tried to withdraw their money. More than 130 banks failed. Riots broke out. Within a week, the panic had spread west to San Francisco. California Governor James Gillette declared a bank holiday on October 31, 1907, and some banks began offering paper currency—scornfully known as "funny money"—instead of the gold they did not have.

Bank of Italy had gold. A. P. spread the word among his customers that they could withdraw their savings at any time in the currency of their choice. Just as he had done at the bank on the wharf, A. P. placed the gold conspicuously behind the tellers' windows for all to see. He wanted the gold to be available to skittish customers who insisted on it. At the same time, he knew that fewer customers would insist on gold if they could see it. While 16 other San Francisco banks failed, Bank of Italy came through the Panic of 1907 with a renewed reputation for dependability. For the second time, the bank had weathered a crisis with cash and confidence.

The Panic of 1907 highlighted some glaring weaknesses in the banking industry. To prevent similar panics in the future, new laws were created. Bank examiners would have to review lending practices and reserves more frequently. Bankers would not be allowed to lend money to family and friends who did not qualify for loans. Eventually, Congress would create the Federal Reserve System, a central bank to help manage the supply of money for the entire nation.

Local customers, as usual, were mainly concerned about the supply of money at their neighborhood banks. Two years after the devastating earthquake, Bank of Italy moved into new granite and limestone headquarters at the intersection of Clay and Montgomery Streets. One of the first big buildings to be completed, the structure was nine stories tall. Even more impressive to San Franciscans who had lived through the earthquake, the steel construction was fireproof.

XIII

EXPANDING THE BANK

October 12, 1909
Columbus Day Parade
San Jose, California

Smiling broadly, A. P. shook as many hands as he could. San Jose had grown since he had lived there as a boy. The city bustled with 50,000 people now. Most of them worked in growing, packaging, and transporting fruits and vegetables from the rich farmland nearby. Within ten years, California would grow more than two-thirds of the produce for the entire country, and San Jose was the busiest fruit packing and distributing center in the state.

Columbus Day, a celebration of the European discovery of the Americas, was a holiday for most workers and schoolchildren. Many celebrated by attending a parade downtown. A. P. met lots of people there who spoke Italian or had Italian names. The annual festivities were particularly symbolic and popular with them because Christopher Columbus was also an Italian, a native son whose explorations had changed history. However, it was not the parade or a desire to see his old hometown that had drawn A. P. back to San Jose. It was a bank.

Two weeks earlier, A. P. had received an unexpected visit from a vice president of Commercial and Savings, San Jose's oldest and largest bank. It was in trouble. The former president had made many sizable loans to his family and friends, and they had failed to repay the money. Now the bank was at risk of going out of business. Did A. P. want the buy it?

He did, for a bargain price. On November 18, 1909, A. P. opened the doors to his first bank outside of San Francisco. He gained the good will of local customers by rehiring the tellers from Commercial and Savings instead of bringing in outsiders. He appointed local business, community, and ethnic leaders to an advisory board to help guide the bank and bring in new customers. He charged lower interest rates than his competitors. He kept the bank open in the evenings and on Saturdays so it would be convenient for working people to use.

A. P. hoped the Italians in San Jose would use his bank, but he wanted other customers, too. So, unlike other bankers of his time, he advertised.

San Jose Mercury and Herald
November 14, 1909

The new institution is to pay special attention to the affairs of people who speak English with difficulty and will have employees who speak the French, Italian, Spanish, and Portuguese languages.

A. P. began by focusing on the banking needs of immigrants as he had done in San Francisco. He wanted working-class people to feel comfortable in his bank. Most banks had marble pillars and fancy ceilings to impress rich customers and scare off any poor ones. Tellers hid behind barred windows to prevent someone from reaching in and stealing the money, and the managers worked in private, locked offices. At Bank of Italy, employees worked in the open where it was easy for customers to see and approach them. The decoration and furnishings were designed to blend in with the neighborhood. Especially in poorer communities, A. P. believed a bank should be simple, sturdy, and orderly.

In a surprising move, A. P. asked his brother, Attilio, to manage the San Jose branch. Attilio was only four years younger than A. P., but they had led very different lives. While A. P. worked on the wharfs, Attilio finished high school. While A. P. negotiated contracts with farmers, Attilio graduated from the University of California. While A. P. led the campaign against Boss Buckley, Attilio treated patients in the Philippines during the Spanish-American War. While A. P. started Bank of Italy, Attilio began a successful medical practice back in San Francisco, caring for patients during a smallpox epidemic and serving on the city's board of supervisors.

A. P. believed that his hard work and earnings for the family produce business had made Attilio's schooling and profession possible. Attilio believed that he had achieved success through his own efforts and abilities. Each brother complained about the other and felt misunderstood and underappreciated. In spite of this brotherly rivalry, A. P. trusted Attilio's judgment and offered him a position at Bank of Italy. In 1907, Attilio left medicine to join his brother's business.

The San Jose branch of Bank of Italy attracted hundreds of new customers in the first days it was open. Encouraged by this success, A. P. looked for other opportunities to expand. He wanted his bank to have branches all over California. Branches could offer the services and resources of big city banks to small communities. If bad weather caused crops to fail in one area, the bank could shift money from other branches to help. Customers would not be at the mercy of local conditions.

Bank of Italy, about 1925
San Mateo Public Library Digital Archives Collection

In the next year, A. P. opened several additional branches nearby. With four branches in San Francisco, one in San Mateo, and one in San Jose, A. P. had created a fifty-mile Bank of Italy chain. In 1913, James and Samuel Fugazi joined the board of directors at Bank of Italy, less than a decade after A. P. had resigned abruptly from the board at their father's bank, Columbus Savings and Loan.

Bank of Italy's expansion did not happen by accident. A. P. was a hard-driving businessman who routinely worked fifteen-hour days. He was also a husband and father who reserved Sunday dinners as sacred family time. After the noon meal, A. P. often suggested an afternoon car ride together. Once underway, he might steer the car, coincidentally, toward a promising location for a new bank. Occasionally he wandered too far afield on these scouting trips, and the family had to spend the night crowded into a single room of a small-town motel. The children sometimes whined and complained, but A. P. never did.

XIV

Invading Los Angeles

Los Angeles, California
1913

In 1900, Los Angeles seemed like an unlikely place for a large city to develop. It lay inland with no natural harbor or adequate water supply, and its prospects for growth appeared limited. Looking past these constraints, ambitious and imaginative city promoters set out to alter nature.

In order to take advantage of the growing shipping industry, why not bring a harbor to Los Angeles? In 1906, the city annexed a strip of land connecting it to the coast at San Pedro, and the Port of Los Angeles was born. It would be ready when the Panama Canal opened in 1914, allowing for quicker and cheaper shipping from the Atlantic Ocean to the Pacific.

If a canal could be carved through Panama, why not redirect a river through California? The Los Angeles Aqueduct, completed in 1913, rerouted annual mountain snowmelt more than 200 miles across mountains and desert to the thirsty city. With enough muscle and will—not to mention loans—nothing seemed impossible in Southern California.

Unlike San Francisco, which was surrounded on three sides by water, Los Angeles could expand north, south, and east. It annexed land in every direction, increasing both its geographical size and its population. Soon after the discovery of oil in 1909, Los Angeles was producing millions of barrels of oil every year in addition to tons of citrus fruit and other agricultural products. Many people moved to Los Angeles in search of good, steady work. Some needed loans to get started in a new place. Others came to retire, bringing their life savings with them. With plenty of land, jobs, and sunshine, Los Angeles was poised to become a powerhouse on the West Coast. A. P. liked the looks of it.

Los Angeles did not like the looks of him. In 1913, the city was inhabited by a largely white, Midwestern, and Protestant population. It was one of the least diverse cities in California. The arrival of an Italian Catholic from a rival city to the north did not inspire confidence or gratitude as it had in ethnic neighborhoods in San Francisco.

Los Angeles Daily Tribune
May 2, 1913

Italians Take Over Park Bank

Worse, Los Angeles already was home to 39 different banks. It did not need another. A. P. set out to get a toehold for Bank of Italy in Los Angeles anyway. He bought the struggling Park Bank and converted it into a branch of Bank of Italy. Local newspaper headlines reflected the general opinion in Los Angeles that foreigners were invading from the North.

Competing bankers and some civic leaders objected strongly. They spread the word that doing business with Bank of Italy was risky and unpatriotic. The usual rumors about A. P. working for the Pope or the mafia resurfaced. A. P. ignored them and advertised to try to attract new depositors. He even posted a sign in the bank window to publicize the staff's fluency in seven different languages.

Tobopn Ce Cphckn; Govori Se Hrvatski;
On parle français; Si parla italiano;
Se habla español; Man spricht Deutsch;
Ome Laoymai Emhnika.

In spite of these efforts, A. P. had little success. The bank lost customers and deposits. After five months, it was in serious trouble. Local opposition to the new bank combined with depressed farm prices and the prospect of war in Europe caused a sharp drop in deposits. Bank of Italy's directors worried that A. P. had made an expensive mistake.

Instead of giving up, A. P. responded by announcing his intention to move the bank to a more prominent location at Seventh and Broadway, near the downtown shopping district. He paid four times as much rent for this new address as he had paid for the old. The directors were horrified. Realizing that they had lost confidence in his judgment, A. P. offered to resign and pay back the bank's losses.

A. P.'s unwavering conviction and willingness to back the Los Angeles branch with his own money stunned the directors. At their next meeting, they refused his resignation and voted to support his plan. A. P. did not bother to attend this meeting. As usual, he was at work, trying to turn his fragile footing in Los

Angeles into something more permanent. He was there to stay. He did not mention retiring again.

XV

From Suffrage to Savings Accounts

June 27, 1921
One Powell Street
San Francisco

As he straightened the flower pinned to his suit coat, A. P. whistled a tune from the opera *Madame Butterfly* by the popular Italian composer Puccini. A. P. paced the new bank, inspecting the couches and curtains. Everything was in order. The five members of the staff were standing at their teller windows or seated at their desks. All the bank needed was women coming in the door, looking for a bank of their own.

Just ten months earlier, Tennessee had become the final state required to ratify the 19th Amendment to the Constitution. After decades of petitions and pickets, women had won suffrage, the right to vote. Until 1920, women had no legal voice in government. They were dependent on their husbands and fathers, brothers and sons to represent their interests in public life. Men controlled not only elections but also the rights to buy and sell property and to make contracts. According to the beliefs of the day, women were not capable of the rational and analytical thinking required for important decisions about money.

As usual, Bank of Italy conducted business outside the constraints of conventional wisdom. Times were changing, and A. P. knew it. He believed that women who could vote also would demand greater choice and independence in managing their own money. He saw a great untapped base of customers in this half of the population, and he wanted Bank of Italy to be the first to welcome them at the only bank in the nation run entirely by and for women.

Other banks had tried to cater to women, usually by reserving one teller window where an employee would assist them with deposits, withdrawals, or financial advice. This system worked for existing customers, but it did not draw in large numbers of new ones. A. P. envisioned attracting women customers on an entirely different scale. With his usual dramatic flair, he selected a prominent and symbolic place to begin. He dedicated an entire upper floor of the bank's new headquarters in downtown San Francisco as a Women's Bank. Its sole purpose was to promote the economic independence of women.

A. P. set out to create an inviting atmosphere for the customers he wanted. The bank was attractively decorated and filled with flowers. More important, he made sure that the women customers in front of the counter were welcomed by women employees behind it. A. P. appointed a woman to manage the bank.

Some customers did not know how to write their names. The staff helped them to sign their checks with thumb prints. One new customer signed her check with A. P. Giannini's name instead of her own. The staff explained that she was the owner of the account and the only person who could sign to release the funds. In a friendly and professional way, the staff taught any customers who were unfamiliar with banking how to do it. The bank offered a full range of services to help women save, borrow, and invest wisely. Staff members taught evening classes to instruct women on business and money matters.

A. P.'s efforts paid off. By 1923, only two years after it opened, the Women's Bank had 10,000 customers and $1.5 million in deposits. It had generated more than $5 million in business transactions including wills, trusts, deeds, and investments. The staff increased to 12 in order to accommodate the growing demand for more and different services. In addition to receiving deposits, the Women's Bank also financed women's projects. It provided money to build a 12-story building for a women's club in San Francisco as well as a large women's athletic club in Los Angeles. The Women's Bank was so successful that A. P. opened a second branch in Los Angeles. Women's organizations across the country praised this pioneering bank and its forward-thinking leader.

XVI

Outgrowing North Beach

June 30, 1921
One Powell Street
San Francisco

The Women's Bank was not the only noteworthy feature of Bank of Italy's new seven-story headquarters. The vault itself commanded everyone's attention. Made entirely of steel and concrete, it weighed fifty tons and was the showpiece of the public grand opening. Over three days, more than 70,000 people streamed inside the white granite building for guided tours. They were impressed both by what they saw and by what they did not see. Although the bank was as elegant as its neighbors, A. P. had no private office. He had no personal secretary and answered his own phone. He sat at a desk on the open floor, ready to meet with any customer who wanted to see him.

With 200,000 depositors, A. P. had built the largest bank west of Chicago, but he did not want his success to alienate the fishermen and dock workers who were his long-time clients. Although the new headquarters was less than a mile outside of

North Beach, A. P. could have isolated himself and left the past behind. Instead, he brought some of North Beach downtown, including Chairman of the Board Pop Scatena and Vice President Armando Pedrini, the bank's first cashier.

A. P. planned to expand into the city of Sacramento, about 80 miles northeast of San Francisco. He knew the area well from his days in the produce business. Although other California banks were expanding, Bank of Italy was growing faster than any of them. Independent bankers, in particular, were alarmed by the bank's rapid growth. Competitors spread rumors hinting that Bank of Italy was undemocratic, un-American, and unsafe. More than five hundred of them joined together to fight the spread of the Bank of Italy within the state. They promised never to sell their banks to A. P., no matter how much money he offered. They spent time at the state capitol urging legislators to limit Bank of Italy's growth.

Independent bankers had reason to fear A. P. He was uncommonly aggressive and persistent. He muscled his way into new towns without regard for existing banks or local business practices. Sometimes the owners of struggling banks asked A. P. to buy them out so they could avoid the scandal of failure. Other times, A. P. approached owners and offered to buy their banks. If they were reluctant, A. P. might offer more money. He believed that in the long run, he could earn that money back and more. With his commanding height, thundering voice, and forceful personality, A. P. could be persuasive and even intimidating.

If he was unsuccessful in encouraging bank owners to sell to him, A. P. was willing to badger and bluff his way to a deal. Once he made several offers to buy a small-town bank, but the owner refused to sell. Determined to acquire this bank if possible, A. P. and an assistant drove to the town and parked their car across the street from the bank. A. P. asked the assistant to get out of the car and walk back and forth as if measuring distances with his feet. When the owner noticed this strange behavior, he came outside to ask what the assistant was doing. He said that Bank of Italy was planning to open a branch at this corner. Faced with the prospect of direct competition with A. P., the owner sold.

A. P.'s high-pressure tactics made other bankers resentful and angry. His network of 41 banks gave him resources few competitors could match. He had more money to loan, and he offered loans at lower interest rates. He increased the number of customers by actively seeking out ethnic minorities in every community. He established departments within the bank to work with potential customers who were Italian, Russian, Portuguese, Greek, Mexican, and Chinese. His list of potential customers overlooked no one and specifically targeted respected leaders in the community such as doctors and priests. A. P. directed his sales people to help potential customers find jobs, translate documents, and register for citizenship classes. His ferocious work habits kept him at his desk from 7 a.m. until 9 or 10 p.m. every night. He could see as many as a hundred customers a day. Who could compete with such a man?

That was the problem, A. P.'s competitors argued. They could no longer compete with Bank of Italy because it had grown so large and powerful. If it could not be checked by competitors, it would have to be checked by government regulators.

Banks had to apply for permission to open new branches. Charles Stern, the superintendent of banking for California, began refusing applications from Bank of Italy. He charged that the bank's hasty expansion had resulted in sloppy bookkeeping and unsound banking practices. Mr. Stern noted that some unwise loans were approved, and overdue loans were not always collected promptly. He believed that the bank published overly optimistic reports of its earnings. A. P.'s reputation for financial wizardry was damaged by accusations of exaggeration and trickery.

Some of the accusations were true. Rapid expansion had caused turmoil in bookkeeping, and local branch employees sometimes approved questionable loans or made other decisions that were at odds with the best interests of the bank. A. P.'s single-minded desire to build a banking empire blinded him to legitimate concerns about the bank. At the same time, he felt unfairly singled out for hostile restrictions. Quick to view anyone who opposed him as an enemy, A. P. believed he was a victim of a conspiracy rather than a powerful player in a high-stakes game. He never forgot old wounds, and his craving for respect and acceptance fueled ever-greater expansionist dreams.

XVII

Joining the Wall Street Club

October 17, 1929
Pacific Union Club
1000 California Street
San Francisco

High on Nob Hill with a view of San Francisco Bay, the Pacific Union Club occupied a historic mansion that had been badly damaged during the fires after the 1906 earthquake. The mansion was rebuilt, and the club resumed its role as one of the oldest and most influential gathering places in the city for prominent businessmen and politicians. Its members included the sons and grandsons of some of the city's earliest millionaires and self-made men. Women were not permitted as members. Apparently, neither were upstart Italian bankers.

Early in his career, A. P. had applied for membership in the Pacific Union Club. With his grand ambitions, extraordinary work ethic, and proven record of success, he was clearly a rising star in the city. Club members with established fortunes may have found

A. P.'s obvious striving to be vulgar and uncouth, or perhaps even an uncomfortable reminder of their own not-too-distant past. They may have preferred the appearance of effortlessness in business and in life. When they voted on prospective new members, they selected only like-minded applicants. A. P. was not one of them.

A. P. did not need a calendar of lengthy lunches with the wealthy elite of San Francisco. He was too busy for card games or afternoons of idle talk. The club held few attractions for him except the one that really mattered: respect. He wanted to assume a visible seat among the city's leading businessmen, and he wanted them to acknowledge and accept him. When A. P. approached, he wanted the best doors in San Francisco to swing open. The doors of the Pacific Union Club snapped shut.

Deeply stung by this rejection, A. P. fought back in the only way he knew. He went to work, more determined than ever to prove himself the equal of any self-made man or his heirs. A. P. wanted his bank to be known and respected in San Francisco and throughout California, but he was not content to stop there. The banking capital of the nation was 3,000 miles away in New York City. The biggest and most powerful banks in the country had headquarters there on Wall Street. Never one to think small, A. P. wanted Bank of Italy to stand beside them, and he saw no reason it should not.

New York bankers could think of plenty of reasons that A. P. and his democratic bank should not stand anywhere near them. They were not pleased at the prospect of an ex-fruit peddler joining their select ranks. They did not like A. P.'s Italian last name, Catholic religion, or California farm roots. They did not like his policy of serving small investors as well as large ones. They thought that A. P. was undignified because he advertised his bank. They believed that his ways of doing business diminished the profession of banking by changing a hallmark of wealth into a neighborhood service. They viewed western banks as risky and unreliable, certainly not the equals of established Wall Street banking firms such as J. P. Morgan & Company.

A. P. believed his principles were sound, and he set out to prove his point in New York. By 1920, there were 800,000 Italian immigrants who had settled there in the congested neighborhoods of Brooklyn, the Bronx, and Manhattan's Lower East Side. This Italian population alone was almost twice as big as the entire city of San Francisco.

As early as 1913, A. P. had sent Armando Pedrini to New York to negotiate the purchase of a bank, East River National. The sellers were interested in having A. P. run the bank, but they insisted that he move to New York to do it himself. A. P. did not want to leave San Francisco, and the deal fell through. In 1919, the same sellers again asked A. P. to buy the bank, and they agreed to let a high-ranking Bank of Italy official come to New York to manage it. This time, A. P. agreed. He would not move to New York himself, but he sent another Giannini, his brother Attilio, to manage the bank for him.

Over the next few years, A. P. bought several other New York banks. In 1928, he even purchased a bank right on Wall Street. The 116-year-old Bank of America had fallen on hard times after years of prosperity. A. P. hoped he could build a network of banks on the East Coast as he had along the West. He merged East River National and his several smaller New York banks with Bank of America. Suddenly, he owned the third largest bank in New York.

As a condition of the purchase of Bank of America, A. P. had promised to keep its president, Edward Delafield. A wealthy New Yorker, he knew more about the ways of Wall Street than the ways of his new boss. Mr. Delafield tried to conduct business as usual from the Bank of America skyscraper on Wall Street. In March of 1929, he turned away a customer who wanted to open a savings account with only $200. When A. P. heard about this incident, he fired off a telegram from San Francisco. "You should take deposits from one dollar up," he wrote. True to his roots, A. P. wanted small investors to be welcomed at all his banks from North Beach to Wall Street.

A. P. related to the underdogs of the world. In spite of the power he attained, he always perceived of himself as one of them. He felt embattled, the object of insults from people whose parents had arrived in America earlier or had achieved success sooner than he had. A history of discrimination made him suspicious and wary, never confident that his success was sufficient.

However, there were some sweet victories. Eventually even the stodgy members of the Pacific Union Club had to admit that A. P. ranked among the most influential businessmen in San Francisco. The formidable doors of the club swung open to him as a full member.

On October 17, 1929, A. P. hosted a dinner for the bank's board of directors and top managers at the club. On this occasion, A. P. marked an anniversary. Twenty-five years earlier, his one-room bank had opened less than a mile away.

The road from North Beach to the Pacific Union Club was longer and more complicated than the grid of city streets would suggest. Of the original nine directors from 1904, only A. P., Pop Scatena, and Armando Pedrini were left. The others had died or retired, and two had resigned. The bank had grown to include 292 branches in small farming towns as well as San Francisco, Los Angeles, and New York City. For A. P., looking out at a commanding view of the city lights from a banquet room at the Pacific Union Club, the future looked brighter than ever.

Two weeks later, the stock market crashed, threatening to erase everything that A. P. had achieved.

XVIII

Hard Times

August 25, 1930
Holy Cross Cemetery
Colma, California

As Pop's coffin was lowered into the ground next to Virginia's older grave, A. P. wept openly. For fifty years, Pop Scatena had been his stepfather, business partner, and advisor. Pop had helped Virginia raise A. P. and his brothers and had taught them to work hard. Pop had given A. P. his first jobs in the produce business and had helped launch his career. In return, A. P. gave Pop a seat on the board of Bank of Italy. Now that seat would have to be filled by someone else.

Pop's burial was a dismal day in a dismal year. In 1930, waves of trouble washed over the nation. The stock market crash the previous fall was only the beginning of the Great Depression, an unprecedented ten-year period of economic hardship. In every region of the nation, people suffered. Many workers lost their jobs and homes. Banks failed, and the hard-earned savings of depositors seemed to evaporate.

Against this backdrop of national concerns, A. P. had problems of his own. He was worried about his son, Mario, and the future of the bank. Mario had worked after school for Bank of Italy since he was a teenager. Early on, A. P. told Mario, "Relatives have to work harder than anyone around here to make good." Mario did. He worked in every department in order to learn for himself how the bank operated. After completing law school, he began his formal career at the bank. He had a brilliant financial mind and a powerful desire to live up to his father's highest ambitions. No one else, not even A. P., knew more about the inner workings of the bank than Mario.

Boarding the *Guilio Cesare* for Europe: (left to right) Mario, Clorinda, A. P., Claire, and Virgil Giannini.
Courtesy of the Library of Congress

In contrast to his nimble mind, Mario's body was stiff and weak. He struggled with hemophilia, an incurable hereditary disease in which even minor cuts or bruises can cause uncontrollable internal bleeding. By his thirties, Mario's legs were permanently damaged. While A. P. went striding about on his great long legs, Mario followed painstakingly with his cane. He sometimes required hospital care to stop episodes of bleeding. Mario compensated for his physical constraints with work habits so relentless that even A. P. told him to ease up.

In addition to Mario's fragile health, A. P. also had been very ill with neuritis, a painful and life-threatening nerve disease, for several years. As his nerves and muscles became inflamed, he could hardly eat, sleep, or walk. Doctors told A. P. that if he did not rest more, he risked becoming crippled or even dying. For a man who had worked 15 hours a day since boyhood, this prescription was bitter medicine.

As his 60th birthday approached, A. P. decided reluctantly that it was time to retire and let someone else oversee his banking empire. A. P. had cultivated talented employees throughout his career. In fact, part of his success had been his ability to recognize the talents of others and give them opportunities to develop. A. P. scheduled job rotations every five years among his top managers. He wanted up-and-coming employees to see that they could be promoted without having to wait for one of their bosses to die. As a result, the bank had a large pool of well-rounded executives who had been trained by A. P. himself.

A. P. liked to reward loyalty, dedication, and performance by promoting people from within his own bank. However, when it came time to announce his replacement, he yielded to a competing goal: his desire to have a nationwide organization. He surprised everyone by naming an outsider, Wall Street banker Elisha Walker, to succeed him. In failing health, A. P. made plans for his life's work to continue without him if necessary.

In that bleak year, there was one bright spot. Bank of Italy continued to expand, and A. P. felt that it had outgrown its name. With more than 250 branches scattered from Oregon to Mexico, in California and New York, his bank was no longer only for Italians, San Franciscans, or even Californians. To reflect his diverse customers and appeal to an even wider range of people, on November 3, 1930, A. P. changed the name to Bank of America National Trust and Savings Association. After 26 years of exceptional service, the Bank of Italy name was retired with honors.

In theory, the new Bank of America could serve all Americans. In fact, quite a few Americans were in no position to make use of any bank. Banks are for extra cash, and many people simply did not have any. In the United States, 1,345 banks failed in 1930. Farm income was lower than it had been in forty years. Business profits across the nation had declined 45-60%. Six million Americans could not find jobs. Under these circumstances, the bank faced difficult challenges, but Elisha Walker would have to address them. A. P. was too ill. He and Clorinda traveled to Austria for an extended rest at a health resort.

In A. P.'s absence, Mr. Walker saw nothing but grim conditions during his first year at the bank. Fewer people deposited money, and many borrowers could not repay their loans. The bank faced a $50 million debt. To cut costs, Mr. Walker laid off 850 workers, but he would have to cut more, much more, in order for the bank to fend off bankruptcy.

In 1931, Mr. Walker proposed selling some parts of Bank of America. They were worth much less than they had been two years earlier, but he felt that he had no choice. A. P.'s dream of nationwide expansion would have to be abandoned in this new and dire economy. The board of directors now included some Walker associates from Wall Street as well as Armando Pedrini and other long-time Bank of Italy employees. The members of the board unanimously supported Mr. Walker's plan.

A. P. did not. Even in his sickbed, he was furious. He was angry that his hand-picked successor to the bank would consider breaking it up and selling it at discount prices. He was unhappy at the prospect of harming his loyal stockholders by providing little or no gain for their investment. He was furious that long-time employees would support their new boss at the expense of what A. P. believed to be their duty to the bank and its stockholders. Suspicious by nature, A. P. believed that Mr. Walker was trying to discredit him and harm his reputation. A. P. was outraged, and for him, outrage was the best medicine. He gathered his strength, got out of bed, and boarded a ship for home.

Some stockholders blamed Elisha Walker for the bank's troubles during the Great Depression. They were worried about the bank's prospects and unsure that Mr. Walker could bring back prosperity or even stability. A committee of stockholders asked A. P. to come out of retirement to take charge of the bank again. Many of the 200,000 stockholders, 6,000 employees, and 1,800 bank board members knew A. P., either personally or by reputation. He had a lifetime of impressive and unlikely accomplishments, and in these hard times, he was the person they wanted in charge.

Energized by this outpouring of confidence, A. P. set out to take back the bank. The first step was for stockholders to vote against the re-election of Elisha Walker and to submit A. P.'s name instead. A. P. rallied his strength for the campaign. At town meetings all over California, he walked the aisles shaking hands and demonstrating his remarkable memory for names. Then he listened and nodded as community leaders and customers told the crowd that the bank was in the hands of greedy outsiders who were earning big salaries and paying golf fees for themselves while their investors lost money. During these fiery speeches, A. P. sat before the audience, a distinguished white-haired veteran of earthquake and fire, panic and prejudice. The speakers reminded the audience that when A. P. was in charge, the stockholders always made money.

For weeks, A. P. traveled to similar meetings and presented himself as a seasoned leader who could restore the bank to its former successes. Then at the annual meeting in Delaware on February 15, 1932, the stockholders elected A. P. as president of Bank of America and Chairman of the Board. It was a landslide victory.

A. P. telegraphed ahead to San Francisco. "Tear down the damn partitions," he demanded, ordering the dividers that the Walker people had installed to be ripped out of the bank headquarters at One Powell Street. He wanted his old desk to be hauled back out onto the floor. A week later at 8 a.m., sixty-one-year-old A. P. was back at that desk, ready to meet with as many customers as he could.

The leadership struggle was costly. It caused a breach between A. P. and some of his oldest associates. He felt betrayed by those who had supported the Walker plan, including Armando Pedrini. Not one to forgive and forget, A. P. regarded these people as traitors he could no longer trust. He cut his ties to these old friends and replaced them on the board of directors.

Back at work, A. P. was confronted by the debt crisis. The bank was in trouble, and replacing Mr. Walker did not solve the fundamental problems of a dismal economy. A. P. worked closely with his brother Attilio, his son Mario, and several other trusted confidantes to cut the bank's expenses. In addition to some layoffs, A. P. proposed a 5% pay cut for most employees and up to 20% for officers with higher salaries. The replacement board members would work for less than half the salaries of their predecessors. A. P. announced that he would work for free.

Forty-one days after A. P.'s return, the bank's deposits stopped dropping and showed a slight gain. It was a beginning.

XIX

BUILDING THE GOLDEN GATE BRIDGE

August 4, 1932
San Francisco

Joseph Strauss, chief engineer for the Golden Gate Bridge District, arrived at Bank of America for an appointment. He took a deep breath, straightened the collar on his shirt, and smoothed his pants while A. P. finished talking with another customer. Then with a handshake and a warm smile, A. P. greeted Mr. Strauss and invited him to sit down. How could Bank of America help him?

Mr. Strauss explained. Several years earlier, officials in six neighboring counties had proposed a bridge to span the opening of San Francisco Bay and connect the city to the northern coast. Voters had approved a $32 million bond to pay for it. Planning began, but designing a suspension bridge that could accommodate great ships, fierce ocean winds, and earthquakes proved more difficult and expensive than anyone had imagined. Some of the structural engineers doubted that it could be done. The project stalled, short on money and support. Mr. Strauss had come to ask A. P. if Bank of America could buy the additional bonds required to begin building.

The completed Golden Gate Bridge.
San Francisco History Center, San Francisco Public Library

A natural mathematician, A. P. did some quick calculations in his head. Although he rarely knew how much money he had in his own bank account, he always knew the numbers that mattered. He knew, also, that numbers alone could not tell the full story. The bridge was an ambitious and high-profile project. Its construction would create immediate jobs and set up long-term opportunities for the region. As a man who had spent years on the wharf, A. P. knew the importance of fast and reliable transportation around the bay for trade and business. If the bridge could be built, San Francisco would benefit, and Bank of America would get some credit.

On the other hand, if A. P. agreed to purchase bonds for a bridge that could not be built, the bank would get plenty of blame, and he would look foolish and irresponsible. He believed that the possible rewards of the bridge outweighed the considerable risk, so he agreed to buy the bonds. Mr. Strauss walked out of the bank with a promise for the money he desperately needed. Construction of the Golden Gate Bridge began five months later.

In spite of this hopeful new project in San Francisco, the nationwide shortages and suffering of the Great Depression continued. A record-breaking drought came to the Midwest and stayed. Heat, insects, and wind destroyed crop after crop. Many people sold or abandoned their farms and looked for work elsewhere. Some moved west to California, hoping for more opportunities there. Few people could afford to buy cars, radios, and other manufactured goods. Factories slowed down or closed, and some businesses failed. Some banks did, also, when too many customers were unable to repay their loans. Uneasy depositors withdrew their savings, leaving banks with even less money.

A. P. wanted to get people back to work and put California's industries back on track. In addition to the Golden Gate Bridge, he invested bank money in bonds to fund other major construction projects like schools, highways, and dams. The bank advanced money to farmers to help pay for planting and harvesting crops as well as equipment and irrigation expenses. A. P. knew that even in hard times—especially in hard times—people needed to eat, and they needed the dignity of work.

At a time when most bankers were desperately calling in loans, A. P. was determined to be patient. Many borrowers, both individuals and businesses, were slow to repay their loans during the Great Depression because they did not have the cash. A. P. chose to wait for eventual repayment rather than force borrowers into possible bankruptcy. He believed the economy would improve sooner if people were not forced into desperate actions.

He knew, also, that they would feel loyalty to a bank that trusted them. As always, he cultivated long-term customers rather than short-term profits.

In 1932, three years after the stock market crash, economic conditions around the country had gone from bad to worse. Anxious people hoarded whatever money they had, leaving banks shorthanded. A. P. wanted to replace the fear in people's hearts with optimism. With this goal in mind, he sponsored a Back to Good Times campaign featuring a weekly radio program of music and inspirational talks from civic and business leaders. The bank paid for the talks to be printed and distributed free of charge through libraries and other organizations.

A. P. toured each of his bank's branches—now numbering 410—to reassure investors and check local loans. During that year, when cash was scarce and deposits at most banks were shrinking, Bank of America's deposits increased by nearly $100 million. The struggles of the Depression were not over, but A. P. had convinced more customers than ever to bank on him.

XX

LENDING A HAND TO THE SEVEN DWARFS

1937
Hollywood, California

When Walt Disney asked Attilio Giannini for a Bank of America loan to complete a full-length cartoon film called *Little Snow White*, Attilio was skeptical. Who would pay to see a long cartoon about seven dwarfs?

In 1931, Attilio had moved from New York to Los Angeles to oversee Bank of America's loans there. He developed friendships with pioneers in the film industry. Celebrities including Cecil B. DeMille, Will Rogers, Mary Pickford, Howard Hughes, and Douglas Fairbanks served as bank board members or stockholders. Attilio provided loans to launch Columbia Pictures in 1920 and served on its board. He arranged financing for Academy Award-winning films including *The Ten Commandments* (1923), *King Kong* (1933), and eventually *Gone with the Wind* (1939).

Some risks paid off surprisingly well. A Bank of Italy loan for the 1921 film *The Kid*, starring the popular actor Charlie Chaplin, was repaid in full just six weeks after the movie opened. Other films were not as successful. After funding more than one hundred films, Attilio had learned to pick his projects carefully. He decided that *Little Snow White* would not be one of them.

Walt Disney believed in those dwarfs. However, the photography and music, not to mention tens of thousands of drawings, were costly. A perfectionist by nature, Disney was determined to make a top-quality film, but production would have to stop unless he found the money to do it right. He decided to go to San Francisco and plead his case directly to A. P. Quite impressed with Disney's passion and creativity, A. P. loaned him $1.7 million to finish the film. When it earned $22 million in its first nationwide showing, A. P. took great pleasure in pointing out his success to Attilio. A. P. went on to approve loans for Disney's *Dumbo*, *Fantasia*, and *Pinocchio*.

The old rivalry between the brothers still simmered. Attilio was in his element in Hollywood. He liked celebrities, stylish clothes, and elegant parties. A. P.'s business wardrobe consisted of four suits, three pairs of shoes, and a few shirts and ties. He preferred work to fancy social events. Although he did not always appreciate his brother, A. P. did trust Attilio. As relative newcomers in the fiercely competitive and exclusive world of banking, they stuck together. Their different strengths—A. P.'s hard-nosed business sense and Attilio's easy grace in rarified social circles—complemented each other and helped establish the new and important motion picture industry.

Since its beginning, Bank of Italy had made loans to promising new businesses in California. Many other bankers considered investing in motion pictures too risky. Making a movie was expensive, and no one knew in advance if it would be a hit. A. P. was familiar with Hollywood from the days when it was little more than acres of orange trees. He was more comfortable than most of his competitors, especially the ones far away in New York, in taking the chance that the film industry would flourish. By the time it did, A. P. had become the banker to Hollywood.

There were privileges and temptations that came with this role. Once Louis B. Mayer, the head of Metro-Goldwyn-Mayer studios, sent A. P.'s daughter Claire a lifetime gold pass that would allow her to attend any MGM film at any time. Claire was delighted, but A. P. would not allow her to accept such a valuable gift from a customer. He insisted that she send it back. A. P. did not want people to think that Louis Mayer or anyone in the Hollywood studios got special privileges from the bank. He wanted every Bank of America customer, rich or poor, to feel valued. From the beginning, small deposits had fostered his banking empire, and A. P. did not want others to think that he had abandoned the roots that gave it life. If he accepted expensive gifts from wealthy and powerful customers, he would hurt his reputation as a banker to ordinary people. Claire would have to buy her own movie tickets just like everyone else.

By 1941, the bank had outgrown its headquarters at One Powell Street. A. P. selected the site for a new building in the heart of the financial district. Located at 300 Montgomery Street between Pine and California, the twelve-story building would be a five-minute walk from the site of the saloon where the first Bank of Italy had opened thirty-seven years earlier. Clarence Cuneo, Clorinda's brother who had helped A. P. rescue the gold after the 1906 earthquake and fire, supervised construction.

When the building was nearly finished, bank executives urged the 71-year-old A. P. to try one of the private offices on the eleventh story. He hated it. A. P. complained that it was "a gilded cage" with "everything but a canary." In no time, his desk was out on the main floor where he would be ready to meet with customers after the new headquarters formally opened.

The grand opening was scheduled for Tuesday, December 9. On Sunday, December 7, the U. S. Naval Station at Pearl Harbor, Hawaii, was attacked by Japanese bombers.

The next day, President Franklin Roosevelt declared war on Japan.

XXI

Banking on the Home Front

December 19, 1941
San Mateo, California

The dedication of the 300 Montgomery Street building was a somber, subdued event overshadowed by the looming war. Although A. P. did not know it, personal sorrow loomed, as well.

On December 19, Clorinda Giannini had a heart attack at her daughter Claire's home in San Mateo. She died three days later. A. P. was heartbroken. For a time he was lost in grief and depression. After 49 years of marriage, he hated being alone. He threatened to sell the beloved family home and move to an apartment in San Francisco. Eventually Claire and her husband moved in with him, and gradually his mood lifted. A. P. kept a picture of Clorinda on his desk for the rest of his life.

In spite of his great sadness, A. P. could not stay idle for long. There was work to do, and lots of it. Nothing was more healing and healthy for A. P. War meant that California suddenly became a military hub, the last stop for nearly everything and everyone sent to fight the war in the Pacific Ocean. As A. P. toured his branches in California, he saw customers waiting in lines that extended into the streets. Crowds and long waits were especially common near military bases, which were put up quickly to train the many soldiers who were going overseas to fight.

Often thousands of troops would appear almost overnight near a small town. Paso Robles, California, with a population of 3,000 people, was overwhelmed with a nearby camp of 20,000 soldiers. San Luis Obispo, originally a town of 9,000 people, suddenly found another 20,000 living next door. King City, with only 1,800 people, had up to 100,000 people from the Hunter Liggett Military Reservation on its doorstep. These towns were not equipped to cope with so many regular visitors who needed to take care of business.

For A. P., the answer to this problem was obvious: more banks. He wanted to increase the number of his branches. At the direction of Secretary of the Treasury Henry Morgenthau, Jr., banking officials refused his requests. They did not want the war to be a means of expansion for Bank of America. A. P. was frustrated, but not for long. He discovered a clause buried in the Banking Act of 1935 which allowed banks to open seasonal branches to handle a temporary influx of people. This provision was originally intended to cover the two World's Fairs held in San Diego and San Francisco, as well as the annual California State Fair held in Sacramento. However, A. P. figured that the clause could apply to wartime branches, too.

Armed with this rationale, A. P. instructed his branch managers to open temporary branches called "installations" wherever military commanders requested them. It was a simple matter to broach the idea at the base and receive a request for a bank. If the Treasury Department officials were unhappy, they would have to deal with the commander of the base. A. P. could explain that he was merely providing a service requested by the U. S. military during wartime.

As usual, once he had an idea, A. P. did not wait for explicit permission to act on it. He regularly beat out competitors, in part, by taking bold action first and attending to regulations and social niceties later, if necessary. This formula often succeeded, but always at a cost. Banking officials increasingly viewed A. P. as an alarmingly powerful renegade, a man who played by his own rules, often at the expense of his competitors. Secretary Morgenthau, in particular, believed that a man of such insatiable ambition needed to be watched closely and contained when possible.

A. P.'s wartime banking installations undoubtedly performed vital work. Soldiers must be paid, and they have living expenses. During a single month in 1942, A.P.'s installations provided $14 million for salaries and cashed 220,000 checks for military personnel and support staff. In 1943, the Treasury Department reluctantly gave up the fight and approved all of A. P.'s temporary branches. In a time of war, their efficient services were too essential for scruples about inappropriate expansion. The work needed to be done, and Bank of America was ready and willing to do it well.

In one unprecedented and tragic situation, A. P. created new installations at government request. After the attack at Pearl Harbor, Japanese submarines trolled the Pacific off the coast of California. Some people presumed that Imperial Japan's next logical target would be the mainland. They suspected that anyone of Japanese descent living in the United States could be a traitor or spy. Rumors spread along the Pacific shoreline that local Japanese fishermen were setting mines in harbors or that Japanese farmers were poisoning the fruits and vegetables they brought to market.

Soldiers and civilians sandbag the windows of a
downtown hotel to block flying glass and bomb
fragments in the event of a Japanese attack on San
Francisco. The windows have been blacked out to prevent
visibility from the air at night. December 23, 1941.
San Francisco History Center, San Francisco Public Library

Navy demolition experts drag ashore a 12-foot Japanese torpedo
head section near the Golden Gate Bridge. Another section of
the torpedo lies in the lower right foreground.
San Francisco History Center, San Francisco Public Library

The rumors were false, but frightened officials urged that all Japanese on the West Coast be transferred to relocation camps to prevent communication with the enemy that might lead to attack or invasion of the United States. With little advance preparation and no long-term plan, more than 110,000 Japanese, many of them loyal U. S. citizens, were removed from their homes and forced to live in makeshift camps in remote parts of western states for the duration of the war. The United States was also at war with Germany and Italy, but people of German or Italian ancestry—like the Gianninis—were not as easily identified and were not subject to internment.

In June of 1942, the Federal Reserve Bank of San Francisco called for banking services at the Tule Lake and Manzanar relocation camps in California. A. P. did not have to be asked twice. He quickly established part-time installations in the camps, serving the needs of interned Japanese two days a week. A. P. sought out ignored or underserved populations throughout his banking career, but never in such extraordinary and unfortunate conditions as these.

Elsewhere in California, the war brought thousands of new residents. Before 1940, agriculture had brought people to the state. After the Pearl Harbor attack, they came for jobs in the war-related industries that abruptly and profoundly altered the state's economy. Skilled labor for the aircraft plants around Los Angeles and for ship building on the San Francisco Bay created many boom towns. Mare Island Naval Station, one source of tugboats and marines during the 1906 earthquake, served as a vital shipyard for construction, repair, and maintenance of the Pacific fleet and required thousands of workers. San Diego doubled its population, and Los Angeles grew by 800,000 new residents due to wartime manufacturing. Over two million people from other parts of the country poured in during the years just before and during the war.

Ever alert to business opportunities, A. P. knew all these people needed homes and places to save their hard-earned money. The flood of people coming to California would bring many potential bank customers. In addition to individual needs, businesses and industries needed expanded banking services. Many small businesses converted their facilities to make parts for ships, aircraft, guns, tanks, and other machinery necessary for the war effort. Their owners needed loans to retool their factories and to purchase materials. Automobile plants were needed to manufacture tanks. Bathing suit companies shifted to making parachutes. Even Walt Disney got a $1 million loan to switch from animation to educational and propaganda films. Bank of America loans helped many companies make these expensive and complicated changes.

Even so, businesses had to be flexible and creative to survive. Some had to reinvent themselves to meet the needs of changing times. For example, the Solar Aircraft Company of San Diego was a survivor, with a little help. Through the Great Depression, the company had manufactured bookends and frying pans, supported during the lean years with small but timely loans from Bank of America. In 1939, the company requested and received $100,000 to shift to defense manufacturing. During the war, the little company won war contracts worth over $90 million, and Bank of America loaned over $4 million to fund expansion. By 1944, the company was making parts for B-29 bombers. After the war, the company switched to making components for jet airplanes, and Bank of America loaned another $8 million. The bank's decision to support a struggling business during the Depression made a difference as well as a profit.

In this time of turmoil, changes at the bank were inevitable. Most able-bodied men under the age of 40 were drafted to serve in the military during the war. More than a third of the nearly 10,000 bank employees left their jobs in order to serve their country. At the same time, wartime demand for banking services increased. Women made up most of the difference as they took over jobs previously held by men and filled new positions. By 1945, A. P. employed more than 11,500 people to staff his banks. Women comprised half of the bank's employees, a reflection of the growing number who participated in the national work force during the war years.

In spite of the difficulties and shortages, deposits at Bank of America rose sharply during the war. Nearly everyone who was not in uniform was employed. There were fewer goods to spend money on, since gasoline and many other commodities were in short supply or rationed. Total bank deposits at the time of the Pearl Harbor attack were under $2 billion. By the end of the war, they had more than doubled. In good times and bad, A. P.'s bank grew, fueled in part by his relentless search for new customers, new markets, and new roles in a rapidly-evolving world.

XXII

The Peace Dividend

1945
300 Montgomery Street

World War II ended in 1945. A. P. was 75 years old. Although Bank of America was now enormously successful and powerful, A. P. was not content to sit back and rest. He had learned from the 1906 earthquake and fire that opportunity follows closely on the heels of disaster. For four long years, everything the nation could muster had been put into the effort to win a huge global war. Now millions of soldiers were coming home. In anticipation of their return, the United States Congress passed the Servicemen's Readjustment Act of 1944, commonly known as the G. I. Bill of Rights, to help veterans of the war return to civilian life.

Before the war, few average Americans could afford a house or a college education. The G. I. Bill offered veterans inexpensive home or business loans and money for college. That money had to come from somewhere. A. P. made sure that some of it came from Bank of America. By 1949, Bank of America had loaned $600 million to World War II veterans under the G. I. Bill of

Rights. Between 1945 and 1952, the bank processed 78,000 home loans.

The United States was not the only country struggling to reabsorb veterans and recover from the war. In many ways, the war had made the world seem smaller. People had followed the progress of battles in Germany, Russia, the Philippines, tiny islands in the South Pacific, and Japan. Although there were branches of Bank of America in England and in Italy before the war, A. P. felt the time was right to expand his bank in the international community. He opened a branch in Manila, the Philippines, in 1947. He made plans to open branches in China, Thailand, and Guam. Even though Japan had been a bitter wartime enemy, the United States tried to help the country recover from the damage of the war. Bank of America opened branches in Tokyo, Yokohama, Kobe, and Osaka.

All these branches would provide loans to help the people rebuild their homes, businesses, and lives. Additionally, A. P. made sure that his bank conspicuously participated in the Marshall Plan, which provided loans to the Western European nations that had been devastated during the war. To A. P.'s great satisfaction, Bank of America was the leading lender for reconstruction in Italy.

Some people feared that the end of the war would mean a return to the Great Depression with unemployment and hard times ahead. Not A. P. He had great hope for the future and predicted that most of the new people who had come to California during the war would stay. He said, "The West Coast hasn't even started yet." He felt that many items that had been invented during the war years—electronics, television, light metals and products of every kind—would now be developed for peaceful purposes. Jobs would be created to produce new consumer goods. These goods would become more affordable and commonplace.

For instance, A. P. recognized the great potential of the automobile industry. Automobiles had existed since the 1906 earthquake, when the few available cars had been seized by troops to provide emergency services. After World War II, many people moved to the suburbs where cars were essential for transportation. As cars became more affordable, more people wanted to buy them. A. P. was a pioneer in helping people to pay for expensive purchases. Bank of America offered installment plans that allowed customers to buy cars and other goods—stoves, refrigerators, washing machines, vacuum cleaners—by paying a little each month over time. With low rates and efficient service, the bank attracted many customers. In just a few years, only General Motors would finance more car loans than A. P.'s bank.

A. P. himself had very little interest in cars except as a means of efficient transportation. Restless to get wherever he was going, he liked to hop in a car when it was already moving and jump out before it had come to a complete stop. Fortunately, he was happy to have someone else drive, and he hired a series of chauffeurs. Once a driver appeared breathless at headquarters and reported that he had "lost Mr. Giannini." In fact, Mr. Giannini had slipped out of the car a number of blocks back and walked briskly to his office without thinking to inform his driver. A. P.'s interest in cars ended where traffic began. He had a bank to run.

A. P. did not like to waste time when he could be working. He preferred to be shaved by a barber in a shop near the office so that he could be discussing the day's business with executives rather than standing in front of a bathroom mirror at home. He was utterly absorbed in his work.

It was with good reason that work absorbed his full attention. By October, 1945, Bank of America had become the world's largest non-government bank with total assets of over $5 billion. Even the Wall Street bankers who had scorned A. P. could not deny that he was a master at finding and keeping a broad base of customers, now nearly four million strong. Small deposits could bring big profits, after all. Immigrants, farmers, tradespeople, women, and soldiers all could be valuable customers. If other bankers wanted their business, they would have to offer more competitive services to a more diverse population. In an effort to compete with A. P., most did.

XXIII

Retiring Once More

May 6, 1945
San Francisco

A. P. resigned as Chairman of the Board of Bank of America on May 6, 1945. He was given the title of Founder Chairman, a position created especially to honor him. Of course, A. P. had retired before—only to return to work—but he said, "This time I mean it." He promised that in the years ahead, he would serve only as the bank's watch dog, but he vowed, "If I ever hear that any of you are trying to play the big man's game and forgetting the small man, I'll be back in here fighting."

Right or wrong, A. P. believed that he had built the best, most honest, most public-minded bank in the country. It was hard for him to give up the influence and responsibility he had held for so many years. It was hard for the bank's executives, too, and even after his retirement, no important decisions were made without his approval. He was the ultimate authority at meetings he attended, and any seat he took became the head of the table.

A. P. (fourth from right) returns to Alviso in 1925 to hand out
diplomas at a school graduation.
*Reprinted with permission from <u>Alviso, San Jose</u> by Robert Burrill
and Lynn Rogers. Available from the publisher online at <u>www.
arcadiapublishing.com</u> or by calling 888-313-2665*

As founder of the world's largest bank, A. P. became one of
the most powerful people in the world. However, he had no
interest in becoming one of the richest. He studiously avoided
personal wealth. "I don't want to be rich," he said. "No man
actually owns a fortune; it owns him." A. P. believed that "a lot
of people working together can create a lot of wealth for a lot of
people. But one man who works selfishly for his own wealth at
the expense of others creates nothing worth having. He generates
poverty. There's poverty in his mind, in his heart, and in time it
will show up in his pocket."

As the value of his stock in his own bank increased, A. P.
found himself, as he said, "in danger of getting into the millionaire
class." To prevent that possibility, in October of 1945, A. P.

created the Bank of America-Giannini Foundation. Its purpose was to provide educational scholarships to bank employees and to promote medical and scientific research. A. P. donated half his personal fortune to this trust fund and commented, "Our best crop is always these young Americans. It's the only good crop where the land has never failed us, year after year."

Bank of America — Giannini Foundation

"...Administer this Trust generously and nobly, remembering always human suffering... Like St. Francis of Assisi, do good — do not merely theorize about goodness. This is my wish and I confidently commit this Trust to your hands for its fulfillment."

A. P.'s instructions to his son Mario, the executor of his will

In the years after the war, A. P. appeared less frequently at his office. He had suffered from heart trouble for some time, and he developed chronic bronchitis. He celebrated his 79th birthday at home on May 6, 1949, with Mario and Claire and a few close friends. Less than a month later, on June 3, he died in his sleep of heart failure.

Tributes poured in. The *New York Times* said, "No one has had a greater influence on the history of California." The *Los Angeles Times* said, "Money was not an end to him; it was a means. His unorthodox methods have been much criticized, but also much copied." A. P. left an estate valued at $489,278. By today's calculations, he was worth less when he died than before he started the bank.

Mario received many letters from customers and ordinary people. One letter said, "He is the first big business man for whom many people will grieve or shed any tears. While I have the greatest respect for Morgan, Vanderbilt, Rockefeller and our authentic big shots, A. P. was the only one of them who had any sincere interest in the average American or any love for the common people." To him, banking was noble work that allowed him to help other people achieve their dreams. In this process, he achieved his own.

A. P.'s funeral was held in San Francisco at St. Mary's Cathedral on June 6. The church was overflowing with 2,500 people, and thousands more lined the streets to watch the funeral procession. After a brief service, A. P. was buried next to Clorinda at Holy Cross Cemetery in Colma, California. In keeping with his wishes, all Bank of America branches around the world were open that day for business as usual.

Authors' Note

A. P. enjoyed great professional success in his life, but he also suffered devastating personal tragedies. Only three of his eight children lived to adulthood. Both of his surviving sons, Mario and Virgil, suffered from hemophilia and were vulnerable to dangerous uncontrolled bleeding. Virgil, who had held minor positions at the bank, was frail and seriously crippled from this disease. He died at the age of 38 after falling in his apartment and hitting his head.

A. P. considered Mario to be the one who would take his place at the bank. Mario was a studious young man who graduated with highest honors from the University of California at Berkeley and Hastings College of the Law in San Francisco. Though different from his father in personality and style, Mario proved himself a worthy successor. He took a wildly growing collection of banks and molded them into a smoothly functioning branch banking system. He always viewed his accomplishments as minor and gave any credit to his father. Mario did become president of the bank in 1936. He survived his father by only three years before dying at the age of 57.

Claire, A. P.'s only surviving daughter, was born in 1904, the year Bank of Italy opened the door to its first one-room bank in North Beach. She attended Stanford University and married an All-America football player, Clifford "Biff" Hoffman. He had a casual work ethic and a tendency to drink too much, which did not impress A. P. The two men sometimes argued bitterly. Biff died in 1954. His life was marred by alcoholism and unfulfilled ambitions.

In 1949, after A. P.'s death, Claire was appointed to fill his seat on Bank of America's board of directors. She was the first woman to serve there. Claire tried to keep alive her father's concern for maintaining the personal touch between the bank's staff and its customers.

Claire had special concern for women, who by 1954 comprised 60% of all bank employees. Once when she visited a branch bank in Sunnyvale, California, she noticed that the female tellers were always standing. Claire suggested getting some stools so they could sit when there were no customers to serve. The manager replied that stools were not necessary. Claire said nothing. Two days later a large delivery truck arrived with stools for the tellers. Like her father, Claire cared about details.

Since hemophilia is a genetic disease passed through the female line, Claire was a likely carrier. She and Biff had decided not to have children. With the deaths of her mother, father, siblings, and husband, Claire was the lone survivor of the large Giannini family. She died in 1997. The next year, Bank of America merged with NationsBank, and the headquarters moved from San Francisco to Charlotte, North Carolina. It was the end of an era.

GLOSSARY OF FINANCIAL TERMS

Bankruptcy: When an individual does not have enough cash or credit to pay the bills that are due, he or she may have to declare bankruptcy. Bankruptcy legally protects the individual from creditors, but it also damages that person's credit rating and reputation. A person who has declared bankruptcy will have a harder time qualifying for a loan than a person who has repaid all debts on time. Companies and banks also can declare bankruptcy.

Bank Holiday: A bank holiday is the emergency closing of banks, usually by an act of Congress or the President, to prevent a financial crisis.

Bank Examiner: A bank examiner works for the Federal Reserve Bank. His or her job is to make sure that banks follow rules and regulations. For example, a bank must maintain a minimum amount of money to meet expected needs. A bank that fails to meet established lending standards may lose its charter and go out of business.

Bank Failure: Individuals and companies deposit money in banks, and then the banks lend part of that money to others. If too many depositors suddenly want to withdraw their money, the bank may not have sufficient cash available to pay them. A bank fails when it cannot pay its depositors their money and must go out of business. The depositors may lose some or all of their money.

Board of Directors: A board of directors is a group of advisors who are responsible for making important policy decisions in a company or organization. The directors of a company are either elected or appointed. They usually choose one person to be the chairman or chairwoman of the board.

Bond: A bond is a promise to repay borrowed money with interest. Governments sometimes sell bonds to pay for major projects like freeways, schools, or even war. A government bond typically has a fixed interest rate.

Cashier: A cashier is a bank employee who receives and pays out money. Cashiers are sometimes known as tellers.

Collateral: Banks want a guarantee or some kind of security that their loans can be repaid. Collateral is something of value that borrowers promise to give to the bank in case they cannot repay a loan. Collateral can be some land, a house, a car, or valuables like jewelry and art.

Credit: Credit is borrowed money that a person can use to purchase needed or wanted items. This money must be repaid on a set schedule. People who repay their loans on time develop a good credit rating and can qualify for more credit in the future. Credit may be linked to a specific purchase such as a home or car, or it may be more general such as a credit card.

Currency: Currency is any item used for the exchange of goods. Coins (quarters and dimes) and paper money (dollar bills) are well-known examples of currency. In the past, people have used gold and other precious metals, food products, and livestock as currency.

Department of the Treasury: The United States Department of the Treasury manages the government's finances. Its responsibilities include collecting taxes, paying government bills, printing money, and supervising banks.

Deposit: A deposit is money that a person puts in a bank temporarily. The money belongs to the depositor, but the bank may lend it to someone else. Banks generally pay interest to the depositor. They typically pay a higher rate of interest if the depositor agrees to leave the money in the bank for a set period of time. The opposite of a deposit is a loan.

Depositor: A depositor is a person who places money in a bank for safekeeping.

Federal Reserve Bank: The Federal Reserve is the central bank of the United States. It has twelve regional Reserve Banks. The Federal Reserve Bank was created after the Panic of 1907 to help reform banking and smooth the flow of money from one part of the country to another. The Bank of Italy first joined the Federal Reserve in 1919.

Interest: Interest is a fee paid by a borrower to a lender. For example, a person who borrows money from a bank must repay that money plus a fee, usually a small percent of the loan.

Loan: A loan is money borrowed from an individual or bank. It usually has to be repaid with interest by a certain date. The opposite of a loan is a deposit.

Panic: A panic is a financial crisis. Risky investments, a stock market plunge, overdue loans, and bank failure can contribute to a panic. A run on many banks at the same time can create a general financial panic or recession.

Reserves: Reserves are money held by a bank for the purpose of paying customers when they want to withdraw their deposits. The Federal Reserve Bank dictates the amount of reserves a bank must have on hand. The purpose of reserves is to avoid financial panics by having enough cash on hand to serve the bank's customers.

Run on the Bank: A run is a type of financial crisis. It is caused by large numbers of bank customers quickly withdrawing their money because of fears that the bank will fail. A run actually increases the likelihood that a bank will fail by placing extraordinary demands on its reserves.

Stockholder: A stockholder is an individual who buys a piece of a company. The individual pays money for the stock, and the company uses that money to perform or expand its business. If the company is successful, the stock may become more valuable, and the stockholder can sell it for a profit. It the company is not successful, the stock may become less valuable or even worthless. The stockholder may lose money. A stockholder is sometimes known as a shareholder because ownership of a company is measured in shares.

Teller: A teller is a bank employee who receives and pays out money. Tellers are sometimes known as cashiers.

WHAT'S THE BIG DEAL
ABOUT INTEREST?

Try this simple game to see how interest works. Then check your answers on page 131.

<u>What You'll Need:</u>

25 pennies or other small objects

<u>What To Do:</u>

1. Bailey has 10 pennies, Max has 0 pennies, and the bank has 5 pennies. (Make a pile with the right number of pennies for Bailey, Max, and the bank. Also make a pile of 10 pennies for an employer and a place for a college.)
2. Bailey has extra money she doesn't plan to use right away, and so she deposits 5 pennies in the bank. (Bailey gives 5 pennies to the bank.)
3. Max wants to go to college but has no money. He borrows 5 pennies from the bank. (The bank gives 5 pennies to Max.)
4. Max uses all his money to go to college. (Max gives 5 pennies to the college.)
5. Max graduates and gets a job. The employer pays Max 10 pennies. (The employer gives 10 pennies to Max.)
6. Max pays back the bank for the borrowed money (5 pennies) and interest (2 pennies). (Max gives 7 pennies to the bank.)

7. The Bank pays back Bailey her money (5 pennies) and interest (1 penny). (The bank gives 6 pennies to Bailey.)

How many pennies does the bank now have? Bailey? Max?

Notice that the bank charged Max more interest (2 pennies) than it paid Bailey (1 penny). A bank makes money by charging borrowers a higher interest rate than it pays to depositors.

WHICH IS MORE:
DOLLARS OR QUARTERS?

The answer seems obvious until you see how quickly interest can grow. Try this simple game to understand. Then turn to page 131 to check your answer.

<u>What You'll Need:</u>

Paper and pencil or a calculator

<u>What To Do:</u>

Hannah's dad offers to pay her an allowance for doing chores for 10 weeks during the summer. He offers her a choice: he can pay her $5 a week (Plan A) or he can pay her $0.25 the first week and then double her allowance each week (Plan B). Which allowance plan would pay Hannah more money? Use this chart to calculate your answer:

	Allowance Plan A	Allowance Plan B
Week 1	$5	$0.25
Week 2	$5	$0.50
Week 3	$5	$1.00
Week 4	$5	$
Week 5	$5	$
Week 6	$5	$
Week 7	$5	$
Week 8	$5	$
Week 9	$5	$
Week 10	$5	$
Total Summer Earnings	$	$

TIMELINE

The Life of A. P. Giannini	Events in U. S. History

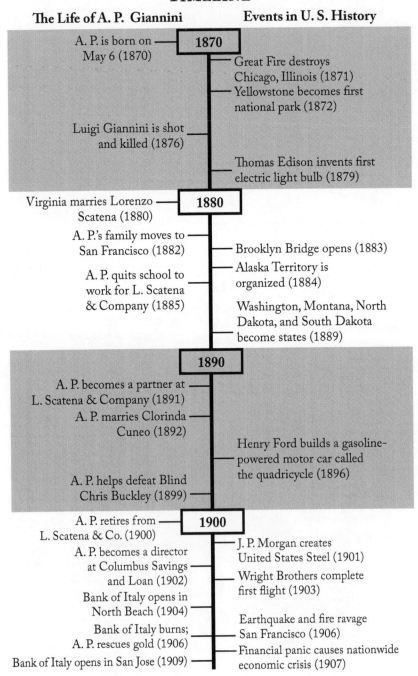

1870

A. P. is born on
May 6 (1870)

Great Fire destroys
Chicago, Illinois (1871)

Yellowstone becomes first
national park (1872)

Luigi Giannini is shot
and killed (1876)

Thomas Edison invents first
electric light bulb (1879)

1880

Virginia marries Lorenzo
Scatena (1880)

A. P.'s family moves to
San Francisco (1882)

Brooklyn Bridge opens (1883)

Alaska Territory is
organized (1884)

A. P. quits school to
work for L. Scatena
& Company (1885)

Washington, Montana, North
Dakota, and South Dakota
become states (1889)

1890

A. P. becomes a partner at
L. Scatena & Company (1891)

A. P. marries Clorinda
Cuneo (1892)

Henry Ford builds a gasoline-
powered motor car called
the quadricycle (1896)

A. P. helps defeat Blind
Chris Buckley (1899)

1900

A. P. retires from
L. Scatena & Co. (1900)

J. P. Morgan creates
United States Steel (1901)

A. P. becomes a director
at Columbus Savings
and Loan (1902)

Wright Brothers complete
first flight (1903)

Bank of Italy opens in
North Beach (1904)

Earthquake and fire ravage
San Francisco (1906)

Bank of Italy burns;
A. P. rescues gold (1906)

Financial panic causes nationwide
economic crisis (1907)

Bank of Italy opens in San Jose (1909)

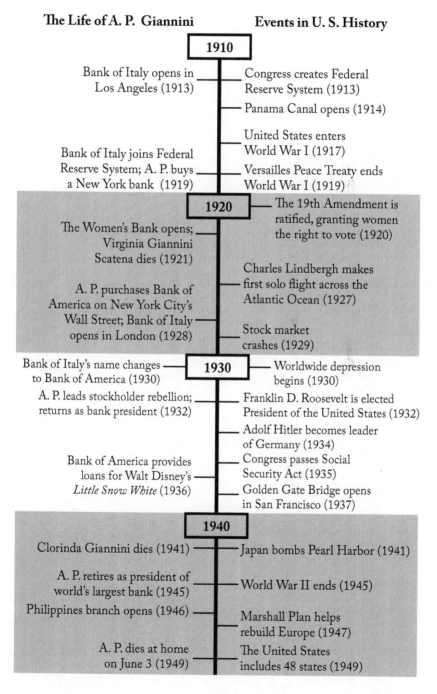

The Life of A. P. Giannini — Events in U. S. History

1910

Bank of Italy opens in Los Angeles (1913) — Congress creates Federal Reserve System (1913)

Panama Canal opens (1914)

United States enters World War I (1917)

Bank of Italy joins Federal Reserve System; A. P. buys a New York bank (1919) — Versailles Peace Treaty ends World War I (1919)

1920 — The 19th Amendment is ratified, granting women the right to vote (1920)

The Women's Bank opens; Virginia Giannini Scatena dies (1921)

Charles Lindbergh makes first solo flight across the Atlantic Ocean (1927)

A. P. purchases Bank of America on New York City's Wall Street; Bank of Italy opens in London (1928)

Stock market crashes (1929)

Bank of Italy's name changes to Bank of America (1930) — **1930** — Worldwide depression begins (1930)

A. P. leads stockholder rebellion; returns as bank president (1932) — Franklin D. Roosevelt is elected President of the United States (1932)

Adolf Hitler becomes leader of Germany (1934)

Congress passes Social Security Act (1935)

Bank of America provides loans for Walt Disney's *Little Snow White* (1936) — Golden Gate Bridge opens in San Francisco (1937)

1940

Clorinda Giannini dies (1941) — Japan bombs Pearl Harbor (1941)

A. P. retires as president of world's largest bank (1945) — World War II ends (1945)

Philippines branch opens (1946)

Marshall Plan helps rebuild Europe (1947)

A. P. dies at home on June 3 (1949) — The United States includes 48 states (1949)

BIBLIOGRAPHY

Note: Every direct quotation in this book comes from one or more of the sources listed in the bibliography.

Arbuckle, Clyde. *Clyde Arbuckle's History of San Jose*. San Jose: Smith McKay Printing Co., Inc., 1985.

Bonadio, Felice. *A. P. Giannini: Banker of America*. Berkeley and Los Angeles: University of California Press, 1994.

Bronson, William. *The Earth Shook, the Sky Burned*. San Francisco: Chronicle Books, 1959.

Burrill, Robert and Rogers, Lynn. *Alviso, San Jose*. San Francisco: Arcadia Books, 2006.

Cinel, Dino. *From Italy to San Francisco*. Stanford: Stanford University Press, 1982.

Dana, Julian. *A. P. Giannini: Giant in the West*. New York: Prentice-Hall, 1947.

Gumina, Deanna Paoli. *The Italians of San Francisco, 1850–1930*. New York: Center for Migration Studies, 1978.

James, Marquis and James, Bessie Rowland. *Biography of a Bank: The Story of Bank of America.* New York: Harper & Brothers, 1954.

Kennedy, John Castillo. *The Great Earthquake and Fire, San Francisco, 1906.* New York: William Morrow & Company, 1963.

Kurzman, Dan. *Disaster! The Great San Francisco Earthquake and Fire of 1906.* New York: William Morrow, 2001.

Nash, Gerald D. *A. P. Giannini and the Bank of America.* Norman: University of Oklahoma Press, 1992.

Rink, Paul. *A. P. Giannini: Building the Bank of America.* Chicago: Encyclopaedia Britannica Press, Inc., 1963.

Smith, Dennis. *San Francisco is Burning.* New York: Viking, 2005.

Thomas, Gordon and Witts, Max M. *The San Francisco Earthquake.* New York: Stein and Day, 1971.

Yeates, Fred. *The Gentle Giant.* San Francisco: Bank of America N. T. & S. A., 1954.

Weidlinger, Tom. American Experience: The Great San Francisco Earthquake. WGBH Educational Foundation, 2005.

WEBSITES

The Virtual Museum of the City of San Francisco (www. sfmuseum.net)

San Francisco Public Library Historical Photograph Collection (sfpl.lib.ca.us)

Bancroft Library, University of California, Berkeley (bancroft. berkeley.edu/collections/earthquakeandfire/index2.html)

ANSWERS

What's the Big Deal about Interest?

Answer: The bank has 6 pennies. Bailey has 11 pennies. Max has 3 pennies. Both the bank and Bailey earned money by receiving interest. Max lost money by paying interest. However, Max now has a college education that may help him earn more money in the future.

Which is More: Dollars or Quarters?

Answer: Plan B. Doubling the payment is the same as getting 100% interest. Note how quickly it adds up. Plan A earns $50 (10 weeks x $5). Plan B earns $255.75. Hannah's dad may want to rethink this offer!

4735377

Made in the USA
Lexington, KY
24 February 2010